Nicole Lynn Snyder lives in a small town in Northeast Tennessee with her daughter and three pets. She started writing after facing a traumatic experience that forever changed her life. Writing brings her an extreme happiness she had never expected. She lives every day crunching as much time as possible with her daughter, who brings light to everything she does. She lives each day like it is an adventure; never taking for granted the blessings she has received.

To the sunshine in my life.

Nicole Lynn Snyder

THE YELLOW DOOR

AUSTIN MACAULEY PUBLISHERS™

LONDON • CAMBRIDGE • NEW YORK • SHARJAH

Ordering Information:
Quantity sales: special discounts are available on quantity purchases by corporations, associations, and others. For details, contact the publisher at the address below.

Publisher's Cataloging-in-Publication data
Snyder, Nicole Lynn
The Yellow Door

ISBN 9781641823531 (Paperback)
ISBN 9781641823548 (Hardback)
ISBN 9781641823555 (E-Book)

The main category of the book— FICTION / Crime

www.austinmacauley.com/us

First Published (2018)
Austin Macauley Publishers LLC
40 Wall Street, 28th Floor
New York, NY 10005
USA

mail-usa@austinmacauley.com
+1 (646) 5125767

This is the story of a young woman who is taken from her family and dumped into the sex trafficking trade. We follow her story and that of the individuals who enter her life during and after her capture. We have snapshots into her past that help define who she is today and where she will potentially go. This story is written with the intent of becoming a trilogy, so it is left with multiple cliff-hangers at the end.

I am also writing under a pen name. Nicole (my daughter's middle name), Lynn (my mother's middle name), and Snyder (my grandmother's last name).

I have only ever dabbled at writing. An inspirational poem here, a college paper there. However, I was in a car accident and my entire world got flipped upside down. On one of the days after my accident, I started writing. What I am submitting is the culmination of that effort.

She ran as fast as her legs could carry her. Her lungs were burning and the pain in her shoulder was overwhelming, but she kept running. She could hear shouts behind her which pushed her to run faster and farther than she realized she was even capable of doing. She noticed she could hear someone behind her, close on her heels. Suddenly, her body was slammed to the ground by someone tackling her from behind. Before she even had time to scream for Athena, a hand was clamped over her mouth.

Chapter 1

"Hope! It's time for school!"

"Mom, I told you, I have no intention of attending a school where women are forced to wear skirts as a part of the uniform. Do you not see the inequality of being forced into a specific type of clothing simply because you had the misfortune of being born female?" *Why is it that I have to repeat this to Mom every day? Does she not listen to what I say? I deserve respect and she should show it to me!*

Sighing slightly at the repeat in the conversation they had been having for weeks, Faith responded as kindly and firmly as she could muster, without showing her impatience, "You were made aware that this school requires uniforms. You were okay with the uniforms and inequality, as you now see it, before you started hanging out with some of your new friends. Make a decision. Go to this highly prestigious private school that you requested and wear the uniforms, or the bus will be here for the public school down the road in about 15."

"Public school!" Hope shrieked. "Wait, the bus? Why would I take the bus? I have a car right outside that I can use. No way am I taking a filthy bus to school." She vehemently shook her head in denial. As she spun on her heel to leave the room, Faith's voice reached her ears.

"The car was the agreement upon you going to that private school you selected. Not a public school. You made the decision, now you'll live with the consequence. What's it gonna be, Hope?"

"You are impossible, and I hate you!"

"You are perfection, and I love you." Faith could not understand this sudden change in Hope. It seemed like every time she turned around a new issue was cropping up, inhibiting her ability to communicate with her beautiful 17-year-old daughter. Watching Hope stomp out of the room, Faith sank into a chair. The strength she had been showing Hope was no longer there.

At what point do you tell your highly independent and stubborn daughter that you are dying? How long until the wigs you have been wearing finally give her a clue? Will she notice? Or will it be too late and you will have waited too long?

Faith's shoulders sagged as she sat on a stool at the bar in her kitchen. Surrounded by as much normalcy as she could provide Hope without revealing the real reason for their move: breast cancer. The doctors back home had not been able to help her. It was time to go to a specialist, they had said. A specialist? *So that instead of my doctor, who has known me for years, a stranger could tell me I had three to six months?*

Stomping into the room, Hope dropped her backpack onto the counter next to Faith. Spinning on her toes, she displayed her uniform to Faith. The red, white, and black plaid skirt, topped by a white button-up, which was flattering to her slight frame. Faith sighed internally, seeing the womanly curves the uniform could not hide; half-tempted to agree with Hope on the inappropriateness of a young lady in a skirt.

"Better, Mother?" Hope sarcastically asked.

"Beautiful and strong and smart," Faith replied with all the strength and reassurance she could muster.

"Oh, yay," Hope replied in disgust. "Mother dearest gives her stamp of approval." *She is doing it again. Sitting here like she is so dejected and unloved. Like she is the one who will be going to this dreadful school.*

"I am sorry this bothers you so much, Hope. I did my best to involve you in the conversation so that you would feel included. If you are unhappy with the choice you made, we can enroll you in the public school instead." Faith could not help hoping she would choose the public school. Then she thought of the outfits Hope could end up in at that school. Hope's outburst interrupted her thoughts.

"I hate you! You never listen to me! I am trying to explain to you why being forced to wear a skirt because I am female is inappropriate! Can you not see that? Or are you so caught up in how this move has only affected you?" Hope, by now, had stomped her way to the door, slipped on her ballet flats, and opened the door. "I wish I never had to see you again!" she slammed the door with all the strength she could muster.

The door shook on its frame from the force of it slamming. On the other side of the door, Hope hesitated. What if those were the last words she said to her mom? No, she was being dramatic. No way was she going back in there.

Inside, Faith once again slumped in her chair, then gave up and laid her head down on her arms, the coolness from the marble countertop chilling her.

Four hours later, she woke to the sound of a knock on her front door. Disoriented, she realized she had fallen asleep on the bar stool in the kitchen. A knock sounded again and she realized there was someone at her door. Confused, as they knew no one here. Tugging her light blue shirt down over her black yoga pants, she cautiously crept towards the door. Remembering something she had heard from a friend, she did not go all the way to the door, instead calling, "Who is it?" from the hallway.

"Oasis Glen Police Department," a voice responded.

Confused and concerned, Faith crossed the floor quickly to open the door to a man in uniform. He presented his badge. "Officer Smith," he stated. "We found a 2014 yellow Honda Accord abandoned on the side of the road this afternoon. It is registered to Faith Matthews," he said referring to the notepad in his hand. "Is that you?"

Faith felt her entire world tilt on its axis. "Yes, that is my daughter's car. I am Faith." Completely bewildered, she asked, "Was my daughter not with the car?"

Huffing slightly, the officer reiterated that the car had been found abandoned. Faith felt as though she were hearing all of this from the end of a tunnel. The officer emphasized the word abandoned again. "We have had the car towed here. Will you accept the charges from the tow company?" he asked. Nodding mutely, Faith signed a paper accepting responsibility for the car. The officer turned to signal to the tow truck driver to unload the car. He then proceeded to tear off a ticket and handed it to Faith for illegal parking on the side of the road.

Faith looked from the ticket to the officer and asked again, "Where is my daughter, officer? Have you found her yet?"

The officer shook his head slightly, face concerned, then stepped back realizing he was only here to drop off the car. He had been given strict orders to drop off the car and to leave. "No, ma'am. Have a good day." Tipping his hat, he left the front porch and headed to his patrol car. Faith immediately turned and ran to her phone. Calling the phone number on the refrigerator for Hope's school, Faith waited impatiently for someone to answer.

"Ashley Prep School, this is Melody, can I help you?"

"Hello Melody, my name is Faith Matthews, mother to Hope Matthews. I need to speak to her as quickly as possible, please, it's an emergency," Faith stated as calmly as she could. She felt her voice waver on the please but knew she needed to hear Hope's voice to ensure that she would be okay. Two minutes later, Melody came back to the phone. "Ma'am, this is Melody. Unfortunately, we are not showing that Hope made it to class this morning. Were you not calling in to say she was sick?"

"No, no, I'm not. I just had an officer show up to my front door with her car. Can you please double check to make sure that she did not make it to her class?"

"I am sorry, ma'am. It is a small classroom; she definitely did not make it to school today. I am being called away to a meeting, please let me know if there is anything that we can do to help. I am sure she will show up back home in no time." The phone clicked in Faith's ear. Aghast at having been hung up on, she quickly looked up the phone number for the public school down the road.

"Oasis Glen High School, can I help you?" a woman's voice answered.

"Hello, my name is Faith Matthews, my daughter and I just recently moved to this area, and she was deciding between you and one other school. I know we registered at the other school, however, she and I had a conversation this morning about the potential of her attending your school instead. By any chance, did she happen to come to your school this morning for class?"

An exasperated sigh came across the line. "Please hold."

Faith immediately lost her temper. "This is not something that you get to just put me on hold over. I cannot find my daughter, please do not put me on hold." School band music proceeded to play over the phone. She had been put on hold, despite her request to the contrary. Seething, she waited for five minutes before giving up and hanging up. Calling back, she heard, "Oasis Glen High School, can I help you?"

Slowly calming her breathing, Faith began, "Hello, I am a benefactor to the local private school and I would like to extend the same invitation to you. I have a blank check here in front of me and I am hoping to speak to someone who can help me figure out what number to put on this check. May I speak to the principal perhaps?"

"Absolutely! One moment please, let me transfer you," the woman said excitedly.

She heard a brief beeping and then heard the phone connect. "Hello ma'am, Teresa informed me that you are calling to make a donation to our school…"

"No, actually, let me interrupt you before any more time is wasted. I called your school ten minutes ago and was placed on hold while I was looking for my daughter. I am trying to determine if a new student showed up today. It is an emergency and your staff felt it was necessary to put me on hold," Faith spoke very firmly, attempting to curb the anger she was feeling.

"Wow, okay, ma'am. I am extremely embarrassed. My name is Karen, I would be more than happy to help you with this. What is your daughter's name and what does she look like?" Principal Karen responded quickly.

"She's gorgeous," Faith responded. "Her name is Hope Matthews. She is five-feet-seven-inches, weighs 122 pounds. She has honey-cream blonde hair that goes approximately to her waist, soft, wavy curls. She has green eyes like you wouldn't believe. They look like emeralds. She was wearing an Ashley Prep uniform when she left the house this morning."

"I am more than happy to help you in whatever way I can, I am a mother of four and I would be devastated if I ever lost one of mine." Karen reassured.

"Thank you," Faith breathed.

Hours later, night had fallen. Faith had driven up and down every road she could and called all of Hope's friends. She was exhausted and completely haggard. No one had seen her. No one knew where she was. She called the OGPD, and they informed her that they could not create a missing person's report for 24 hours. Driving to the spot where they had found her car, she walked up and down looking for some sign of what could have happened to Hope. As she was glancing down, she saw something shiny. Walking over to it, she saw a small pool of blood. Hand going to her mouth, Faith collapsed on her knees sobbing. Something had happened to Hope, she did not just run away.

Four months later, you would not even recognize the woman on the screen. The woman who had not seen or heard from her daughter in four horrible months. The gauntness of her face contrasting sharply with the fire in her eyes. She wore purple for Hope. To show Hope that she would not forget about her. She would never stop looking. She just needed more time! Time. A relative term. She was not even certain how long she had. She had foregone the last two chemotherapy treatments because they made her too weak to continue her search for Hope. On top of that, she was not getting better. There was no point pretending she could prolong the inevitable.

With her hair pinned in a simple French twist, to cover the pins in the wig, Faith found her voice. The black pants and purple shirt were a testament to her determination that she was still the strong mother Hope needed.

Stepping up to the microphone, she took a deep, calming breath and began, "This started off with the officers saying that my daughter was a simple runaway; telling me that my daughter was a normal 17-year-old. One who would run away because they didn't get the nail polish color of their choice. Or the school of their choice." Faith felt her voice waver and she stepped back to clear her throat. The police chief standing by her side grew red in the face at the beginning of her speech. He

14

started to lean in to take over. Faith saw a hand reach out and pull his shoulder back. She did not know who it was, but she was ready to continue and would not be silenced. Catching a woman's eye in the crowd, she saw her main support system for the past few months: Principal Karen. Karen nodded her head in encouragement. Feeling her strength and determination return, Faith continued.

"A simple runaway. A contradictory statement said without the compassion or understanding of someone who has lost someone before. Lumping my daughter in without any understanding of what a normal teenager is. For if the police chief had a teenager, he would realize that there is nothing normal about a teenager.

"There is a misconception that everyone can be fit or lumped into a specific category based on gender, age, demographic, education level, etc. Now it has been brought to our attention that Hope wasn't just a simple runaway. Why? Is it because they listened to her mother? Was it because she showed back up, safe? No. It's because she was seen. An undercover cop, or so it is being spun now, found her in a brothel."

A gasp skittered across the crowd and the police chief quickly pulled Faith aside, taking over the microphone stating that none of this was confirmed and there would be no further statements or questions. He was a tall, broad-shouldered man. His grip strong and brown eyes hard as he glared at Faith. He ran a hand through his brown hair, scattering the tips of his military cut with his exasperation and anger. The scar starting at the top of his left eye and running down his cheek bright white in stark contrast to the red of his face.

Faith, aghast at being pulled out of the way, stumbled down the stairs of the stage, terrified that there would be legal repercussions. Do they not understand? They needed to recognize that there were 12 missing girls in the last six months and nothing was being said. Nothing was being done. Faith refused to let Hope be another statistic.

To have this many teenage girls go missing and have them not do anything about it was ludicrous!

Faith was almost to her car when she felt a hand grip her shoulder and spin her around, slamming her into her car's door. His height dwarfing Faith as she stood pinned to her car.

"What the hell do you think you're doing?" yelled the chief. "Have you lost your damn mind? Do you realize the damage you just did to this case? All in your self-righteousness…"

"You're hurting me. Let go," Faith calmly interrupted.

Upon her words, the chief proceeded to grip her shoulder even tighter, digging in. Faith's legs started to crumple beneath her. The pain radiating through her body was so intense and she was so exhausted that her vision started to fade. She looked desperately behind the chief and saw no one coming to her rescue. She started to scream. The chief immediately backhanded her and she crumpled to the ground.

When Faith came to, she was sitting in her driver's seat with her seatbelt fastened with the car not running. She was drenched in sweat, the 90-degree temperature outside blasting down on her black car. The seats absorbing the heat and radiating it into her. Panic immediately set in. She started clamoring to get out of the car as quickly as possible. Adrenaline coursed through her and she felt a flash of dread as she realized that the car was locked and she could not open the door.

She immediately pulled the lock and shoved the door as hard as she could with her shoulder, crying out in pain when the door did not open. Looking in her side-view mirrors, she saw that each of her doors had been dented and jammed closed.

Desperation consumed Faith. She frantically tried unbuckling her seatbelt to be able to try and get loose and get out of the car, only it too was jammed. That is when she saw a cruiser start driving slowly by the car. She immediately slammed her hand on the horn, desperate to get help. She watched in horror as a hand reached out the window and dropped her keys and purse. Realization struck. She would not be getting out of her car.

Chapter 2

A few miles away, a woman lay on a bed, feet chained to the leg posts and arms tied with silk ropes to the headboard. Her hair, silky brown with red highlights, making it look like the most beautiful mahogany wood, was swept to the side of her head with her curls cascading down. Her eyes held a jarring luminescence in the dark room as they shone like emeralds in the faint light. The blush, high on her cheeks, was there naturally, as well as the red hue of her lips. The red and black lace corset accentuated young yet lovely curves. Her chest was rising and falling quickly as her anticipation rose. Waiting for him to enter the room. Wondering where he would start. Wondering if the assorted toys of pain and pleasure on the wall would be used, as they often were.

She arches off the bed, testing the movement allowed by the restraints. The chains at the end of the bed that are attached to her ankles begin to rattle as she moves. Their sound breaks the extreme silence in the room. After the sound, she immediately stills and listens for movement on the other side of the door. Straining to hear, her breath becomes more shallow and fast, hoping for some sign of another person. After what feels like an eternity, she starts to relax, thinking perhaps it would not be tonight. Suddenly, a knock sounds at the door and her whole body tenses.

A man enters the room, eyes raking down her body as he sees the prone position the beautiful woman is in. He saunters to the bed, where he stands to take in the view. He turns slightly and sees a woman standing at the door. He tilts his head sideways, not daring to use his voice or show his masked face. Covering only the top half of his face, the black mask eerily contrasted with the white of his face.

"Does she please you?" the woman queried.

The man leans down and roughly grabs the corseted woman's chin and turns it from side to side. He glances back at the woman at the door and grins maliciously. He stalks back to the door and shuts it forcefully, indicating that he was not to be disturbed. He immediately strode then to the wall, pulled off the whip, and brought it to the bed.

On the other side of the door, the woman heard the whip snap and the sound of a scream.

Chuckling softly, she moves down the hall as sounds of terror and cries come from each of the rooms.

"Take it well, Hope. Take it well."

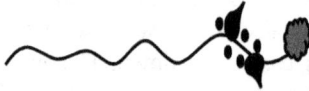

She reaches her office, where the opulence is overwhelming. Maroon brocaded couches on both sides of the room, next to the walls. The difference: they were facing the walls, not the inside of the room, as one would expect. On side tables on both ends of the couch were boxes of tissues with trash cans underneath. While checking to see if everything was as it should be, a discreet knock sounded at the door. Ten seconds passed before the door opened. A man entered the room nodding his head at the woman.

Striding directly to the couch on the left wall, he proceeded to pull a hidden lever that turned the wall next to the couch into a one-way window. On the other side of the window, a young girl, approximately 12 years old, lay prone over a spanking bench. Hands chained to the floor, eyes blindfolded. A man and woman stood over the child. One with a whip, the other with a paddle. They took turns hitting the child before stopping to kiss passionately.

At the sound of a zipper being pulled down, the woman in the office glanced to the man drawing down his zipper and then left the room using a hidden door at the back. Walking briskly to her desk, she sat down before dozens of cameras. All showing each of the rooms in the brothel as well as the hallways.

She chuckled slightly at the bald man sitting just on the other side of the wall, noticing in passing that he seemed to have put on a little weight. She could see him furiously working himself and quickly switched her gaze to the other screens. Seeing each of the rooms full and men waiting in the lobby and viewing rooms, she almost missed when one of the rooms was empty. Checking the hallways, she saw Hope slung over the shoulder of the man she had just left with her. He was walking swiftly to the back door.

Quickly rushing from her office, she saw the man putting himself away and throwing away used tissues. Nodding curtly, she ran from the room, dropping to a steady pace upon reaching the hallway. Catching up quickly to the man with his burden, it was then that she saw the damage done to Hope. Blood dripped from her to the back of the man's suit, some landing on the floor. The black carpet quickly hiding the red color.

"What have you done to my merchandise?" she hissed.

Turning quickly at her words, he stumbled and almost dropped Hope. Glaring, he continued with her close at his heels. Finding a back door, he pushed his way through, knocking Hope's head against the frame. When she made no sound, the woman realized that she was either dead or unconscious.

"Get rid of her." She watched as he took off down the street, dropping her behind some dumpsters before pulling out his cell phone. A limousine pulled up and he climbed in quickly before the car raced into the night. Turning, she gasped when she saw that the man from her office had followed her.

"I'll handle this, ma'am," he said confidently as he pulled a badge from his pocket and placed it on his chest.

Starting to head to the dumpster, he stopped when he saw another man approach the girl and kneel down next to her before pulling out his phone. Presumably he was calling the police. Watching to see what he would do, he waited about two minutes until the sound of sirens touched his ears. At the sound, the man next to the girl ran away, disappearing into the night. Waiting for other officers to fill the scene, the man from the brothel walked down the alley, blending into a group of officers.

Chapter 3

When she came to, all she saw were white walls. There was an incessant beeping that had finally roused her. She did not understand where she was or why she was there. Glancing down, she saw bandages on her hands and arms and an IV sticking out of her left arm. She did her best to remember where she was and if she had gotten there herself or someone had brought her. She tensed as she heard the door open and saw a woman walk in.

"You're awake! It's great to see those beautiful green eyes of yours."

The woman who walked in wore purple scrubs with an array of butterflies on the scrub top. Her smile was bright and genuine. "My name is Nicole, and you are at the Plumeria Hospital here in Oasis Glen." Grabbing the chart at the end of the bed, she smiled warmly before continuing. "I am a nurse here and will be helping you out for the next eight hours or so until my shift ends. Then I will introduce you to Jelissa, who will take over at that time. She's a lot nicer than I am." She chuckled softly to herself as she said these things.

Trying to rise up in bed and open her mouth to speak, Nicole quickly admonished her. "You need to rest, your throat must be extremely raw. We know who you are, Faith, your face has been plastered all over the news. First with your speech about that brothel, now most think you're making that part up, and then about you being trapped in your car. Now, it's being spun that you tried to commit suicide over the grief of your daughter," Nicole prattled on.

Faith gasped at this. *Grief over my daughter? Did they find her? Is she dead?* Panic set in thinking that she had lost her before she could tell her she loved her and was proud of her.

She needed to tell her to not worry about what she had said when she left that day. She needed to give Hope the letters she had written for her about what she had done for these four months while she had been missing. Swallowing rapidly, Faith whispered, "Is she…?" she could not say it. Could not say that she was gone.

"Oh, sweetheart, no, she hasn't been found yet," Nicole said reassuringly. Faith breathed a sigh of relief. No way would she ever give up on Hope. Someone must believe her. "Now, sweetheart, we need to focus more on you," Nicole started.

Faith attempted to speak again. Her voice, though scratchy, worked enough to say two words, "What happened?"

Nicole looked up, startled by the question. Moving in closer, she sat in the chair beside the bed. "Sweetheart, we were hoping you could tell us. You have been unconscious for almost 12 hours now. A man called in, said you were unconscious in your car, completely unresponsive."

As Nicole spoke, Faith started being flooded with memories. The heat, the terror, the desperation. She felt so out of control about the ability to help herself. Despite being in the hospital, she was immediately transported back to that feeling of helplessness in her car. "He locked me in. He hit me, then he locked me in my car!" Her voice raspy. Nicole thought she had misheard her.

"Wait, you're saying that the man who called in about you being trapped hit you, and put you in that car? I saw the bruise on your face and thought that maybe when he broke in the window…"

Faith immediately shook her head in the negative, then regretted the sudden movement. "Broke the window? I don't…" Faith hesitated here and attempted to clear her throat. It felt like gravel had lodged in her throat and she had lost the ability to speak. She gestured helplessly at Nicole, unable to speak anymore.

Nicole immediately climbed up on the bed, sat next to her, and gave her a hug. This woman, who had never met Faith before, showed such a capacity for love and understanding that Faith was overwhelmed. With tears, she sobbed with every fiber of her being, knowing that someone was here to listen, and for once she did not have to do this alone. She cried until she could not cry anymore, then she felt the weight of her dread settle on her and fell into a tormented sleep.

Waking later to a darker room, she felt a hand on her shoulder, it was Nicole. "Hello Faith sweetheart, I'm sorry I woke you, but I promised that I'd introduce you to Jelissa before I left for the night." A woman with beautiful caramel skin walked in, hesitating briefly when she saw Faith. She walked over to the side of the bed, then immediately leaned down and enveloped Faith in a warm hug. "I look terrible, don't I?" Faith rasped.

"You look beautiful," both Nicole and Jelissa countered. Their skin tones so completely opposite each other's, making a sharp contrast as they stood staring down at Faith. Both their gazes were so full of understanding and compassion that Faith felt her throat tighten and a single tear slipped down her cheek.

"Let it out, sweetheart," Nicole said softly. "I'll be back in about 12 hours. You're in amazing hands."

Faith reached out her hand and grasped Nicole's. "Thank you," she struggled to say.

"Before I go, I am going to give you a little bit of pain medicine to help you rest. You've been murmuring in your sleep and I know you're not feeling rested. You need your rest, so you can heal faster and get back to finding your beautiful daughter," Nicole gently said.

"All right, honey. I'm gonna take over now. You and me, we're gonna get nice and personal tonight, if you're up for it." Jelissa smiled upon the completion of her statement. Nicole's laugh sounded of little bells as she walked out. The stricken look on Faith's face relaxed as she realized Jelissa was teasing her. "I'm thinking you'd quite enjoy having your face and hair washed. Does that sound okay to you?" Jelissa queried gently.

Panicking, Faith started to say no, but the thought of her face being washed sounded perfect. Jelissa would find out soon enough that her hair was simply a wig. One which would probably have to go into the trash. Faith nodded gratefully. "Perfect! I love the personal nights," Jelissa teased. She turned to review Faith's chart.

Faith then realized what was happening. Neither were treating her as a victim, rather they were treating her as a woman who had been hurt but was not helpless, was not defenseless, and was definitely not alone. For a moment, Faith took comfort in knowing that she was not going to have to go through this alone. Then she was swamped with guilt. Hope was alone. She did not have anyone supporting her, loving her, or hugging her. It was not fair that she, as the parent, had the support, and not her beautiful daughter.

"Faith, none of this is your fault. You do know that, right?" Jelissa quizzically asked. Shaking her head fervently, Faith suddenly felt the whole world sway and then the nausea rise. Jelissa, recognizing the look, immediately grabbed a bucket so that Faith could empty the contents of her stomach into it. Seeing blood, Faith desperately wanted to hide her face from Jelissa. When Jelissa saw her embarrassment, she immediately looked in the bucket. Seeing blood, she hastened from the room to grab a doctor.

Faith sank down into her pillows and started shivering. The months that she had been given to live through this cancer were going down faster than she had thought. A doctor entered the room, speaking in hushed tones with Jelissa. Jelissa gasped and covered her mouth with her hand, turning her head to look at Faith, eyes shimmering with tears, she knew she could not let fall.

Faith was transported back to the day she had been told. The memory was so vivid, it felt like it was yesterday. She had been fighting the cancer for over a year. Today, she would find out if she was the winner or if cancer was. The doctor calmly entered the room, his glasses perched on his nose. The Santa look always made Faith smile and relax. "Well, Faith, I decided to do something a little different today. Normally, I would have reviewed the results and tests before coming in here. However, today I wanted to review them with you. Is that acceptable to you?"

"Of course, yes. Thank you for being willing to do this together, it means a lot." Faith replied gratefully.

Flipping open the manila folder to view the results, the doctor walked around his desk to take a seat beside Faith. "Well, Faith, let's take a look. Based off of your white blood cell count and your…"

"Faith!" Jelissa yelled. "Are you okay?" Her face completely filled with concern as she leaned towards Faith's bed.

Seeing the doctor standing next to Jelissa, she realized that her cancer was no longer a secret. "He told you my prognosis," Faith gasped.

Jelissa silently nodded. "You're dying." As she moved to step over to Faith's bed, there was a loud commotion in the hallway, and a gurney was rushed past with a frail woman in a shredded red and black corset. Her body lay bruised and broken. A crash cart was called for and Jelissa and the doctor rushed from the room. Faith silently sent up a prayer that the young woman would be okay and fell into deep sleep as the pain medication Nicole had given her before leaving finally kicked in.

Chapter 4

While Faith was plagued by nightmares in her room, Hope lay battered and bruised in the adjacent room. Doctors and nurses were frantically trying to determine the extent of the damage done. The blood and bruises covering her body amazed the doctors that she was still alive. The sound of the heart monitor flat-lining stopped everyone in their tracks. Then, frantic movement ensued as they raced to get a crash cart into the room. By unspoken agreement, they all decided that they would not be losing this woman tonight.

They immediately placed the paddles on her chest and started to use them when they realized that her corset would be made of metal. As quickly as they could, they sheared off the remaining tattered clothing, some nurses gasped as they saw the bruises, welts, and scabs from prior abuse. Jelissa immediately grabbed a sheet as they placed the paddles on her chest. Shocking her four times before the monitor registered a heartbeat. Then, frantic movement resumed as everyone tried to help.

Frustrated, Jelissa realized that there were too many hands, which could lead to mistakes. Quickly, she started assigning nurses and doctors alike to other tasks, asking them to check in every hour to see who would need a reprieve. Jelissa started a chart to catalogue all the injuries this poor woman had endured. The bruising, gashes, and swelling made her features impossible to see. The woman had no form of identification. Jelissa felt like she should know her, but could not figure out why. There were fingerprints on her neck and gashes along every inch of her body. The gashes appeared to be placed there by a whip.

After spending over an hour filling out a chart with all the injuries, Jelissa started to feel overwhelmed. How anyone could hurt someone so mercilessly was beyond her. She had heard that the young woman had been found behind a dumpster, the man who called the police not even sticking around. Jelissa looked back over at the woman. Appalled by what she was seeing, Jelissa excused herself to deal with the officers who had shown up and to find out any other information she could.

Mustering as much authority in her voice as possible, Jelissa addressed the two men in blue standing just inside the waiting room. "Hello officers, my name is Jelissa. Is there any further information you have garnered for the Jane Doe just brought in?"

"For this particular case, we have no need to speak to a nurse. All the information we have will be conveyed to a doctor. Why don't you run along and find one?" intoned one of the officers. Between the balding head, the huge paunch of a stomach, and the stench emanating from him, Jelissa's stomach churned in disgust. Of all things, he smelled of sweat and sex and she could not fathom why.

"Well, Officer, if you have the inability to comprehend information exchanged with a nurse, I'll be happy to find a doctor who can better speak your speed." Jelissa demurred.

A man waiting in the room seemed to chuckle and then cough. When Jelissa slightly turned, she found no one paying any attention. Wrinkling her brow, she turned back to the two officers standing in front of her. Baldy and Ignoramus, she mused to herself. Baldy understood he had been slighted and was none too pleased. Meanwhile, Ignoramus stared with bewilderment at her.

"Why, I thank you kindly, ma'am. That would be mighty fine of ya," Ignoramus drawled. Baldy scowled and stalked away, clearly insulted by the entire exchange. Jelissa turned to leave the room and bumped into a man as he was leaving. Shockingly blue eyes captured her attention before they dropped and he shuffled past. A slight limp to his gait. Strange, she did not know which patient he was here to see, but did not have the time to ponder it, as she needed to check on her other patients. As if on cue, the hospital intercom announced needing Jelissa to come to Room 222 urgently.

Jelissa gasped as she realized that this was Faith's room and she had not checked on her for a few hours. Recognizing her mistake and hoping it was not too late, Jelissa sprinted off towards Faith's room, worry creasing her brow.

Turning the corner, Jelissa saw a uniform leaving Faith's room but could not place who it was. She quickly entered the room and saw that a white pallor had settled over Faith's face. Another nurse stood in the room shaking in terror.

"He had the pillow over her face. He insisted it was him trying to pull the pillow off her face while she fought him, but I know what I saw." The nurse gasped out. "I immediately offered to help and was quickly by her side to pull it off when, suddenly, she stopped fighting and he turned and left the room. I did not see his face. I don't know who he was, Jelissa, I swear!" the nurse said fervently.

Jelissa quickly ran out of the room trying to see where the officer had gone. A man was turning the corner as she left the room but was not in uniform so was quickly dismissed. Looking up and down the hall and seeing no one, Jelissa quickly headed back to Faith's room. She hurried to Faith's side nervously asking, "Faith, can you hear me?"

Faith's eyes had taken on a faraway look. Her focus was on the wall opposite her bed—glazed and completely unfocused. The other nurse in the room was gently talking to Faith, trying to get a reaction. Jelissa stood watching the other nurse try to get some response from Faith. Not seeing any progress, she started to worry. Then she lost her patience. "Faith, you need to snap out of it! You do not have the time, luxury, or privilege to just give up. Hope is out there, alone and afraid. You are the one who needs to help her. No one else is going to care as much as you do."

The other nurse looked completely aghast that Jelissa would dare speak to a patient this way. Shaking her head in disgust, she left the room promising Faith she would get someone to come help.

"Faith, suck it up! Focus on what is important! You are what Hope needs," Jelissa pushed. Grabbing Faith by the shoulders, Jelissa gave her a hard, quick shake.

Color flooded Faith's face and she quickly started to struggle against Jelissa. The nurse ran into the room with a doctor at her heels. Opening his mouth to reprimand Jelissa, he stopped dead in his tracks when he saw recognition cross Faith's face and her crumble into Jelissa's arms.

"You're safe. You're going to be okay." Jelissa crooned.

"Please," Faith gasped out. "Please get an officer and a notepad. I'm ready to tell you what happened." Coughing desperately, she started looking around the room. Jelissa immediately grabbed a plastic cup and straw, filled it with water, and brought the straw to her lips.

"Small sips, honey. I know you'll want to guzzle it down, however, you need to take it slow, okay, Faith?" Jelissa kindly directed.

Faith sipped slowly and then sputtered when her throat rebelled at trying to swallow. She smiled her thanks and took the pen and paper from the other nurse as she walked back in. Baldy and Ignoramus followed.

"I understand that you are ready to talk to us about your attempted suicide," Baldy intoned.

Faith immediately went pale with the knowledge that she was being seen as someone who would give up on her daughter. She wondered what the point was of even trying to talk to this person.

"One word," Jelissa whispered. "Hope. That is why you are doing this. Don't let him detract you from what you are trying to accomplish."

"I didn't say anything," Faith marveled.

"You didn't have to."

Mustering up her courage, and clearing her throat, Faith began. "My name is Faith Matthews, mother of Hope Matthews, and I have been assaulted by the chief of police twice to ensure my silence about the human trafficking occurring in this beautiful town." At this, Faith started coughing profusely. The officers standing in the room looking at her like she had completely lost her mind.

"That is a serious accusation and not one you can make lightly. You need to recognize the consequences of your actions and what happens to those who accuse our chief. Do you understand?" Baldy gravely asked.

"Yah, not cool, ma'am," Ignoramus added.

Jelissa looked at the officers incredulously. "Did you just threaten..." An alarm went off on her watch and she realized it was time to check on her Jane Doe.

"Faith, I need to check on that other patient, will you be okay?" She worriedly chewed her lip.

Faith glanced first at the two officers and then at Jelissa and nodded her head carefully. Jelissa gave the two officers a warning look before leaving the room. Baldy started to step closer to the bed when Faith held up her hand to halt his progress. Quickly, she grabbed her pen.

I am tired now. I will write out a full statement and have someone get it to you. For now, I am choosing to rest. Please see yourself out.

Baldy looked as though he wanted to say more. Rather than doing so, he quickly glanced at his partner and then nodded his head curtly before leaving the room. Ignoramus stared another 20 seconds more at the note before nodding upon completion of reading. Walking to the door, he hesitated long enough to warn, "You stay safe, ma'am."

Chapter 5

Hope walked down a hallway filled with doors. She could see her mom walking ahead of her telling her that she needed to find something or someone. Hope, however, wanted to check every door, certain that her mom could find what she was looking for sooner this way, if only she would let her check. Faith kept saying over and over that she was running out of time and Hope really needed to hurry. Opening each door, she found new memories. The first door on the left, she saw the day her mom had taken her to the park to go down a slide for the first time. She came down way too fast and as she thought she would crash to the ground, her mom scooped her up into her arms and held her safe. A smile came to Hope's face remembering the joy and happiness she felt on that day. There was a man in the background whom she knew was her father, but her memory went no further.

Closing the door, she turned and saw her mom gesturing frantically at her. Holding up a finger to indicate she needed to wait a second, Hope turned to walk a bit down the hall and tried a door on the right. Opening it, she saw a rainy day. She was staring out the window while her father loaded up bags into his car. Her mom was crying and grabbing his arm. She was seven and did not understand what was happening. Remembering that her father would push her mom to the ground, she quickly shut the door so she could move on.

Turning to open another door, she saw boxes packed and her mom standing outside a door at their old house. "Hope, I know you don't want to move, I know you don't want to leave your friends, and I know you hate me right now. I am sorry you are so unhappy about this move, but it is something that must be done," her mom said. Hanging her head, she waited for a reply.

The door opened slowly and Hope saw herself with a tear-streaked face. "Mom, I am scared," she whispered.

"Oh, precious, I know," her mom responded, enveloping her in her arms.

Hope closed the door on the memory, waiting for the resentment she ended up feeling during the move to resurface. When it did not come, she realized just how much her life had changed.

"Hope, I need you to wake up, honey," a voice said behind her. Glancing behind her and seeing no one, she shrugged it off and kept moving forward. The hallway tilted and shook a little suddenly. Hope reached out to steady herself against the wall, discovering another door. She decided this was serendipitous and what her mother sought would be behind that door. Opening it, she saw her mom standing next to the counter in their new house. Guilt coursed through Hope as she stood watching the scene unfold. "Oh, yay, Mother Dearest gives her stamp of approval."

Shame and regret swamp over Hope as she shuts the door. She looks over to find her mom and sees her sitting down the hallway, next to doors with colors. They're no longer the plain white she is used to, but rather there are grays and blues and reds. Curious, Hope goes to the first door and starts to open it when she feels a terrible stinging in her left arm. Looking down and seeing nothing, she quickly grasps the door handle and pushes it open. Immediately, she is consumed by fear as she watches herself pull over her car and walk over to an elderly man on the side of the road whose tire was flat.

"No! Stop! Do not go help him!" she starts screaming to herself. But she cannot stop the memory from happening as she watches the man pretend to drop his wrench. Hope watches herself lean down to pick it up, not realizing that he did not actually drop it, when she suddenly feels and sees the wrench come down on the back of her head. Searing pain crashes through her as she stumbles out of the room. Tears course down her cheeks as she leans against the wall and then slides down to rest her crossed arms on her knees, crying with the pain.

"I don't have much time left, Hope," her mother quietly whispers next to her. "We must find the right door. Please help me find the right door!" her mom is getting frantic now. Hope starts to worry and wants to go more quickly through these doors. Stepping up quickly to the blue door, her mom tries to drag her away but Hope shrugs her off and pulls open the door.

Looking inside, she is confused by the darkness. Not understanding, she feels along the side of the wall, attempting to find a switch when she hears whimpering. Then, the memory crashes over her. The room where they brought the new girls. It was always dark in there. No light or sounds were allowed. All the girls had been stripped of their clothing and were simply told to wait. They were kept in that room for five days without any food. Water was scarce and had to be bargained for. The memory of a man walking in asking for a kiss for a glass of water and the girls all clamoring to get that kiss. Hope saw herself standing calmly and saying, "I'll give you two." It was her fourth day trapped in that room and she had not been given any water yet. The shock when she realized that the kisses would not be simply on her mouth but in locations of his choice brought bile to her mouth. Hope quickly backed out of the room when she saw the man fall to his knees in front of Hope.

Shivering, Hope did her best to forget about that room. She did her best to forget about where she had to kiss a man to get out of that room on the fifth day. Out of that room, lurching down the hallway, she saw her mom leaning against the wall, shoulders sagging.

"Hope, wake up!" a voice said forcefully by her ear. She cringed against the sound, not understanding why her mom was allowing her to be yelled at this way. Suddenly, exhaustion tore through her. However, she knew that she had to keep going to find this door for her mom. Red was her mom's favorite color. Therefore, seeing the red door, she lunged for it, certain that it would be the correct door. The room was dim with velvet curtains draped along the walls, hiding the windows. *The windows with bars on them*, Hope thought fleetingly. Only she did not know how she knew that. There was a wall with paddles, whips, chains, silk rope, and so many other tools for pain or pleasure. Seeing a woman on the bed, Hope stepped closer. As she did, she saw the woman move and heard the chains rattle along the floor and bed. She shivered, despite there being no chill to the air. She watched as the woman in a red and black corset leaned up, straining against the ropes tying her to the bed. Not liking what she was seeing, Hope turned to step back to the door when there was a knock and the door opened. Excited, she turned to say hello to her mom when she saw a man in a tux with a mask on. Hope recoiled from him, though she was not sure why.

He walked intently to the bed and looked at the woman there. Not understanding, she turned to ask what was happening when a woman's voice at the door asked if the woman pleased him. A strange uneasiness settled over Hope as she watched the man grip the woman by the chin and look at her before striding to the door and closing it. He walked quickly back over to the bed and then leaned over to grab a whip off the wall. The woman on the bed whispered, "Please," before being backhanded across the face. Crying out, she tried to rise off the bed as the whip came down across her legs.

A scream broke through her lips and Hope's as well as she watched the man retract his hand and strike the woman on the bed over and over, leaving no exposed skin untouched. Hope fell to the floor and watched as the man struck the woman repeatedly until the skin broke. By now, the woman was sobbing uncontrollably from the pain of her wounds.

The man snarled his disgust and started punching her in the face and chest and stomach trying to get her to stop making noise. Hope watched as the man stopped briefly to catch his breath, noticing that the crying had stopped. As she appeared unconscious, the man quickly unbound her hands and unchained her feet. Hope watched confounded by this as he flipped her over.

"Like new," she heard the man whisper. Confused and terrified, Hope rose to leave the room, when he suddenly picked up the ropes he had just unbound and tied her wrists once again to the headboard and chained her legs to the footboard.

"No!" Hope gasped as she realized what the man was doing. He unzipped the front of his pants and climbed on the bed. Straddling the woman, he immediately started to whip her along her back, rising and falling with his body in perfect synchrony with his hand bearing the whip. Once her entire back was completely shredded, he pulled himself out of his pants and started to enter the woman on the bed. Seeing this, Hope immediately ran from the room as the bile in her mouth became too much. She gasped as she left the room looking everywhere she could for her mom. Needing to see her to tell her what she just saw.

Not finding her mom, Hope curled up on the floor outside the red room, sobbing uncontrollably. As she cried, she thought about the woman's face she had seen on the bed and realized that the woman on that bed had been her. Shocked, disgusted, and filled with shame, Hope began to drift off. She did not want to feel the pain anymore.

Somewhere, a woman's voice shouted, "We're losing her!" *Losing who?* Hope thought to herself as she drifted away. Suddenly, a cold, hard shock raced over her body as she lay there on the cool floor. Fighting it, she felt the cold shock come over her again. Only this time, pain followed. Crying out, she felt like her entire body was on fire. Flames licked up the sides of her body and all over her skin. She wanted the flames off. What had her mom always said to do in times of fire? Stop! Drop! And roll!

Hope started thrashing on the bed as soon as Jelissa entered the room. She had heard her screaming 'No!' A few times and was scared for her. She did not understand what was happening as she raced to the room. She had one part of her mind still concerned for Faith, but she needed to take care of the young woman in this room. She did not know who she was, but she knew she had to help her. Jelissa had also heard the call for 'clear' two times before entering the room and knew that this woman might be giving up the fight. Seeing her thrashing on the bed brought relief, and fear that she would do more damage to herself. Grabbing a needle, she quickly asked if anyone had given pain medication to her. No one had, so she pushed morphine into the IV. Hope screamed as the pain tore through her body. She hurt so bad! Why did she have to come back to this?

Jelissa immediately began grabbing cool, wet towels and placing them over Hope's body. Immediately, tears started streaming down Hope's face as she felt the elusive pain medicine begin working at the edges of her pain. The cool towels brought the burning down to a simmer, allowing her to breathe. Darkness swallowed her as the pain medicine did its job and released the last vestiges of burning pain from her body. Sagging against the hospital bed, Hope fell into a welcome, dreamless sleep.

Jelissa continued working on cleaning up the wounds that Hope had endured. Sickened by everything she was seeing, she tried desperately to work as quickly as possible to get as much taken care of before the young woman woke from her drug-induced sleep. The lacerations on her body would not require stitches and should hopefully not scar. Surprisingly, the lashes looked like they had been inflicted initially lighter and then made gradually stronger.

Working quietly and efficiently, she was startled from her attentiveness by a hand at her elbow.

"Hey sweetheart," Nicole whispered gently. "I hear you've been at this all night. Will you let me help you?"

"Oh, my goodness, Faith!" Jelissa fretted. Moving to put her tools down, her legs gave out and she stumbled from standing so long. Nicole grabbed her around the waist and led her to a chair, easing her down slowly so that the blood and feeling could slowly move back into her legs.

"She's okay, I just came from there. Looks like you've made a lot of progress with this Jane Doe. I've been brought up to speed. Apparently, this is one we are determined to save," Nicole said wryly.

"Yes!" Jelissa responded fiercely. She was prepared to go to battle for this young woman whom she had never met. Turning to give Nicole a piece of her mind, she caught sight of her face. It was filled with compassion and mirth, and Jelissa realized that she had overreacted. "I'm sorry. I know you want to help her, too." The exhaustion was making her say things she knew better than to say. She did not even know what time it was.

"Sweetheart, you're okay. I should know better than to pick on you. You've had an extremely long night." Glancing up at the clock, Jelissa realized it was 10:00 am, and she had no clue when she had last checked on her other patients. Concerned, she would be facing recriminations for not caring for her patients, she moved to get up, when extreme nausea hit her.

Swaying on her feet, she collapsed back down on the chair. "Goodness, I guess I overdid it a little. Can you grab me a quick cup of water, see if that helps?"

"I did one better. Here is a cup of coffee and a doughnut," Nicole beamed.

"You are an absolute angel, thank you so much!" Jelissa gushed.

"I know, just don't tell anyone," Nicole replied winking mischievously. Chuckling softly, Jelissa bit into her doughnut just as the door was pushed slightly open into the room. Nicole and Jelissa sat in silence, concerned that the person was not making themselves known. They sat in complete silence, waiting. The door opened a little wider and a man started to enter. He was almost fully in the room when he saw the two women.

"Excuse me, I didn't realize anyone was in here."

He hastened to leave the room, when Nicole stood and addressed him. "Who are you, and why are you coming into this room. Do you know this woman?"

"No, no, no. I don't know her at all. Must have been the wrong room, I apologize," he said, quickly exiting the room. Nicole turned and chuckled that he was so embarrassed, when Jelissa suddenly stood up, gasping. She had bumped into that same man last night. There was no way he was going to the wrong room. He had been outside Faith's room last night. Why was he now outside of Jane Doe's room saying he was lost? There was no way he was lost. She leapt up and jerked open the door and glanced out. Looking in both directions and not seeing him, she stood in the hallway looking back and forth, concern etched across her features.

"Um, Jelissa?" Nicole questioned. "Are you okay? You look as though you've seen a ghost or something. What is going on?"

"That man, he was here last night, too. I saw him outside of Faith's room as well. I don't understand why he would be coming to both rooms. He seems so familiar, like I've seen him before." Shaking her head to remove the cobwebs she felt in her head, she turned and started laughing. "You stole my doughnut."

"What?" Nicole laughed. "You ran out of the room, you looked like you were done with it. What was I supposed to think?" She batted her eyelashes trying to feign a completely innocent expression. It was too much for Jelissa and she leaned against the wall in the hallway, chuckling softly at first and then gradually escalating to a full-blown laugh. Throwing her head back, she continued to laugh. Dropping her head back down to look at Nicole, she had tears of laughter streaming down her face. The grin on Nicole's face and her self-satisfied smirk as she licked off her fingers, caused Jelissa to start laughing again. This time, her mirth was so great that Nicole started laughing as well. Barely able to catch her breath, Jelissa was startled when she heard a voice crying out from the room. "NO! Please stop! Please!"

Racing into the room, Jelissa and Nicole quickly tried soothing Hope. They were at a loss to know how to help her. Their soothing words did not seem to be working, and if they touched her, she either shied away in pain or started thrashing to get away. Hearing a voice in the hallway, they noticed that their Jane Doe started to calm. Not understanding what was happening, Nicole started to speak soothingly once again, "You're okay, sweetheart. You are safe."

The woman started crying out again, "No, please! Not the red one. Do not make me see that again!"

Confused and concerned, Jelissa went out into the hallway to see who had just passed. Presuming it was fellow staff, she hoped that by them coming in, they would be able to help calm the woman. Clearly her tone had connected with Hope in ways that Jelissa and Nicole had been unable to. She was surprised to see Faith in the hallway being pushed in a wheelchair by another nurse, the nurse from last night who had called a doctor to reprimand her. Frustrated, she walked over and relieved the nurse from her duties. Not understanding the flash of anger in the nurse's eyes, Jelissa recoiled from her and grabbed the handles of the wheelchair. Faith turned in her chair and immense relief washed over her face. Not understanding what was happening but feeling as though she needed rescuing, Jelissa started to turn her to take her back to her room.

"Jelissa, it is so good to see you before you leave for the end of your shift this morning. Thank you so much for sending Nicole in there this morning to come see me, that was so very kind of you." She said as cheerfully as possible. Then, under her breath, she added, "And thank you for that timely rescue."

"Rescue? I don't understand, what do you mean by rescue?" Jelissa countered.

"She was taking me to go see the chief of police in a conference room. I said I didn't want to go, but didn't see any way of stopping her. She was quite insistent that…"

"Faith!" Nicole suddenly shouted from the end of the hall. "Can you come here for a minute, please? I want to try something." Jelissa looked at her quizzically, but trusting her, she turned the wheelchair around and started pushing her towards the door where Nicole was leaning out. Jane Doe's room. "I know this is a bit unorthodox, but I wondered if you wouldn't mind coming in here for a minute and just having a conversation with us. I will warn you, this woman has a lot of injuries and it may be difficult to see her. If you do not want to come in here, just say so. But for some reason, your voice seems to sooth her. I need her to calm down so that I can take a better look at her injuries. Unfortunately, with all her thrashing, she is reopening wounds and I am unable to keep the bleeding under control."

Jelissa was surprised by this request, because it was also against hospital policy. However, she quickly pushed Faith into the room after Faith had nodded her consent. Seeing the young woman, Faith immediately started to cry. Silent tears coursed down her cheeks as she sat staring at the beautiful woman someone had decided they needed to break. Then, anger started creeping in and she was prepared for whatever she needed to do. Looking to Nicole, she quickly said, "Tell me what to do."

Nicole was so overwhelmed by Faith's ability to give so generously that she was momentarily stunned. Jelissa stepped in and simply asked her to speak about her day. "Oh, my goodness, this past week has been quite an adventure. One that I never saw myself having. I went to the press conference about finding Hope. I had to decide which wig I was going to wear. Something that said 'Professional mom who isn't going crazy.' Let me tell you, it was difficult." she grinned at this.

Jelissa smiled and interjected, "You looked absolutely lovely. Would you mind terribly if I catch up with you later tonight? My shift is over and I am overcome with exhaustion. I think I may just go sleep in one of the on-call rooms." Faith immediately nodded just as she was enveloped in Jelissa's arms. "Thank you," Jelissa whispered. "You're an amazing woman." Pulling away, Jelissa saw the look of wonder on Faith's face. She stepped through the door in the hallway, catching sight of a man turning the corner with a limp. Without hesitating, she went after him.

Inside the room, Nicole sat down to listen to Faith as she continued the story of her day. "I made sure to wear purple, because that is my Hope's favorite color. She insists that I wear it often. However, I have been more into the golds and oranges lately. Probably because they do not wash out my skin so much. Plus, they look pretty with my current hair choice." Sighing at this, Faith realized there was so much that Hope did not know and began to worry that she may never know these things. With that in mind, she decided to let it all out, "Being diagnosed with cancer was never in my plans. I am 37 years old. I am too young to die. I thought I could beat it. I was so sure that I would be the one who beat the odds. I thought the mastectomy would take care of the problem. Boy, was I wrong. It didn't help. The chemotherapy didn't help either.

For the first week she was gone, I wrote her a letter every morning. I told her everything I wish I'd had the courage to tell her before. I placed them in a box hoping some day she would be able to read them. Every day was a new reminder of how much I missed her. She was, and is, my everything. You never imagine your life without your child. So when it happens, you are at a complete loss." Bringing her hands to her face, she rubbed up and down, the desperation on her face concealed.

Shaking her head realizing that she had drifted off-topic, she glanced at the woman on the hospital bed. Faith noticed that she was resting peacefully. Looking for her cue from Nicole, she wondered if she had done what was needed and needed to go back to her room. She was starting to get exhausted from all the talking and she hadn't slept well worrying about Hope and where she could possibly be. "Nicole,

I am getting extremely tired. Do you think it would be okay to go back to my room now?"

Nicole rose quickly and checked on Jane Doe. Seeing that she seemed to be calm enough, she nodded in affirmation at Faith. Faith became concerned, as Nicole had not said anything since she had started talking. Glancing at Nicole, Faith saw a tear slowly leak out of the side of her eye. Placing her hand on her arm, Faith asked what was wrong. "You're beautiful. Inside and out. You are a woman who has so many things working against you. And yet, without hesitation, you made the decision to come in here and help this woman that you don't know to be able to feel better. You gave of yourself without asking anything in return. It is beautiful and amazing and pure and I am so overwhelmed by your capacity to give. You inspire me to be a better person than I was the day before. You inspire me to find someone new every single day whom I can help. Surely I have something to give as well and I can make the kind of difference that you make in others' lives."

Faith smiled a small, healing smile as she listened to the words she was hearing. "You are already doing everything that I am doing. Do you not realize that, by your very nature, you inspire others to give as much as they can? You give of yourself every single day in a capacity that people do not even begin to understand or appreciate. You take the time to care for me and others who do not have the capability to care for themselves. I knew yesterday when you entered my room that you were going to be someone that I could rely on to care for me. I have no need to feel as though you will not be someone who does the exact same thing for the woman that is lying in here on that bed. Thank you for having the wherewithal and fortitude to be able to care for people as you do."

Nicole leaned down and wrapped Faith in a hug. Both women were overwhelmed by the words they had received from the other. In a while, they had made it back to Faith's room and she rose out of the wheelchair and climbed back up into her bed. She glanced furtively towards the door and then closed her eyes upon seeing no one there.

Hope stood in the hallway seeing only red doors. In every direction she looked, all she saw was the same red door. Doors started opening, showing glimpses of what had happened. She felt the world spinning around faster and faster until she was dizzy, then it only spun faster. She heard her mom's voice faintly in the recesses of her mind and the spinning started to slow. Feeling as though she was finally safe, she started to drift when she realized she could no longer hear her mom's voice. Fear started seeping into her as she realized that her mother was not there with her. As her focus shifted to feeling alone, the flames of pain started covering her body. In the recesses of her mind, she thought she heard someone yell her mother's name. She sought out the source of the sound, hoping to find sanctuary.

Walking down the hallway, she found a door of yellow. She did not remember seeing a yellow door before, but she was sure she could hear her mother's voice beyond it. When she opened the door, all she could see was lush green forest. Anxious that she was not hearing her mom, she started to turn back when she heard her laugh and knew that she had to find where she was. As she got closer to the sound of her voice, she saw a cave lit with sparking crystals and a clear pool of water. There was lush green moss and grass surrounding the pool. It was there that she found her mom. She was sitting on the green blanket of grass chatting away and beckoning to her. Gasping, Hope ran to Faith and collapsed into her harms. She curled up on the grass with her mom, placing her head in her lap. Faith started running her fingers through Hope's hair. Hope listened as Faith told her about her day. She listened until the only sound she heard was the water lapping the sides of the pool and her mother's voice. She finally slept.

Chapter 6

Nicole was sitting at the nurse's station finally getting the opportunity to put her feet up after getting everything done for the day. Between Jane Doe, Faith, and her other patients, she felt she had been going nonstop and her day was not even half-way over. She started to lean down to slip her shoes off when a woman walked up to the desk looking extremely agitated and sad. Her hair was pulled into a messy bun with her auburn fringes framing her face beautifully. Blue eyes were found behind frames with butterflies. Nicole straightened up, hoping she could help her and then slip her shoes off. "May I help you?"

"Hello, yes. I am sorry, I am not usually so out of sorts, but you see, I just saw the news. I am a principal and do not always have the time to catch up on the local news until the weekend. Since it is Saturday, I finally thought I'd get caught up, when I saw the news. I couldn't believe what they were saying about her. She is not that type of person and I do not understand what led them to believe she would ever do something so silly."

"I am sorry, ma'am, but you've lost me. You watched the news and now need medical attention?" Nicole queried. Realizing belatedly that this was rude, she grimaced.

Laughter filled the hallway when Nicole finished asking the question, only it was not from the woman in front of her. Turning, she saw Faith leaning against her door frame with absolute pleasure on her face. "Faith! You're okay! I was so worried about you! Why would you go and do something that was going to worry me so much?" the woman asked.

Sobering quickly, Faith looked at the woman and tilted her head to the side before responding, "Karen, how about you get over here and we can hash it out. After you explain to me why you have balloons that say 'it's a girl.'" Nicole glanced back and forth between the two women. Seeing that Faith felt comfortable, she went back to her main concern and took off her shoes. "Nicole, would you be so kind as to go grab us some coffees?" Faith asked.

Nicole quickly glanced up and saw the teasing grin on Faith's face. "I thought you were serious for a moment and I was cursing the day I called you friend. I am going to sit here and relax. I mean I am going to sit here and watch your door and make sure you and your friend have the opportunity for a nice, long chat," Nicole declared with as much false bravado as she could muster.

Karen started laughing as she walked to Faith's room. "Nicole, if someone has a girl," she leaned her head towards the balloons, "feel free." Turning back to Faith, she shrugged. "What? They were cute. Oh, and I like her," she said just as the door closed. Nicole immediately pulled out the latest romance novel she was reading from her purse and immersed herself in a good read.

Karen followed Faith into her room and carefully shut the door. "Okay, seriously, you have a lot of explaining to do, so get comfortable. But before we get into all that, get over here!" Wrapping her arms around Faith's shoulders, she squeezed really tightly, then started to step back. "Take the wig off, Faith, it looks extremely uncomfortable and I don't want you distracted with discomfort while you are telling me exactly what happened and what drove you to spill that news about the brothel on national television. Your first opportunity to be included in an actual press conference on Hope's disappearance and you immediately chose to share the ace hidden up your sleeve…"

"Two weeks," Faith calmly interrupted.

"Wait a second. What do you mean two weeks?" Karen returned.

"I had a doctor appointment the morning before the press conference. They said the cancer is spreading too quickly. They told me to take the time I had and do something amazing with my life before I go. So, I decided to get as many people aware of this awful sex trafficking ring as I could. I also wrote out a statement last night describing how the chief of police is involved in the ring and how he assaulted me not once but twice…"

"Whoa, whoa, whoa! What are you talking about?" Karen began. Shaking her head, she followed up with, "Wow, I just sounded like my students."

Smiling softly, Faith climbed up onto her bed and relaxed against the pillows. Karen, seeing this, realized just how haggard and tired Faith looked and felt a pang of unease course through her. Pulling up a chair to the edge of the bed, Karen sat down slowly as Faith filled her in on everything that had happened in the last 24 hours. Sitting there listening to Faith, Karen realized that this could be one of the last conversations she ever had with the woman who had touched her heart so deeply.

Nicole was so immersed in her book that she almost did not hear the page calling to Room 272. Realizing that this was the Jane Doe room, she quickly rose from her desk and started to walk there when she stopped to slide her shoes back on. While she bent to slip the shoes on, she did not see the man who slipped out of Hope's room. She took off at a brisk pace, putting the thought of the highlander and the woman of the future out of her mind. Entering the room, she saw the most beautiful green eyes she had ever seen staring at her.

The emeralds gazing out from the woman's eyes looked so familiar. As she tried to place them, she checked the woman's vitals. The woman did not make a sound as Nicole worked. Merely watching her cautiously. When she did not speak, Nicole decided to see what she would say.

"My name is Nicole. I am a nurse. Do you know your name?" she asked gently.

"Am I allowed to speak here?" the young woman asked.

"Yes, of course you can speak," Nicole responded. Figuring that this woman was simply a 'woman of the night,' she was appalled by the question.

"My mother, Faith Matthews, would it be possible to call her?" she asked fervently.

Gasping, Nicole turned. "Hope? Is that you?" Hope's eyes widened and she nodded her head. "Oh, my goodness! Your mother, she is here! Would you like me to go get her?" Hope's face immediately lit up and she nodded her head vigorously. Nicole immediately left the room and ran to Faith's.

She burst into a room and saw a man sitting in the chair next to Faith's bed. Confused, she turned to Faith and prepared to tell her that Hope was here. She was sleeping, so Nicole leaned forward to wake her gently from her slumber. The man to the right of the bed whispered, "It's too late."

Confused, Nicole started to shake Faith's shoulder to wake her. Not understanding what was happening and why she was not responding, she quickly called a code and doctors and nurses raced in, Jelissa included. Disheveled from the on-call room, she burst into the room looking at Nicole with fear etched all over her face. Seeing the man in the corner, Jelissa saw the bright blue eyes staring back at her. "Don't let him leave," she said to some of the nurses standing there trying to help.

A doctor placed the paddles and tried over and over to bring Faith back. After what seemed like hours but were a mere three minutes, he looked up at the clock. "Time of death, 1:34 pm," he said. Shaking his head, he backed away from the table and turned and left the room. Nicole immediately sank to a chair along the wall and sat staring. The door to the room opened and Karen came in with a couple coffees and a huge smile on her face. Seeing the nurses and doctors exiting the room, she did not understand what had happened until she saw Nicole staring into space and Jelissa standing next to the bed holding Faith's hand with tears coursing down her cheeks.

"No! Please, no! She didn't have enough time! She needed to find Hope!" She went to the bed yelling and screaming at

Faith to wake up and that it was not her time to go. She needed to wake up and find her baby girl. She needed to tell her that she loved her just as she always said that she would. Her cries turned to moans as she realized that her friend would not be coming back. She was gone. Turning to look around the room, she saw Nicole, Jelissa, and the man standing there staring at her. "This cannot be happening. She didn't have enough time."

The man standing in the room leaned forward and laid his hand on Karen's shoulder. Turning to look at him with tears in her eyes, tears matched by him, she shook her head no. "It's okay. She knew," said the man. Nicole, Jelissa, and Karen all stopped to look at him.

"What do you mean 'she knew'?" Jelissa asked.

"I had just left Hope's room when I realized that was her. I needed to speak with Faith, anyway, to see what she knew about this brothel she mentioned this morning. None of this is to leave this room. Is that understood?" he said. The women glanced between each other and then looked back at the young man, nodding mutely.

"I cannot tell you my name and I cannot tell you why I am here. I can only tell you that when I walked in, Faith had just finished getting sick. She was mortified by the intrusion, as she had blood on her mouth and knew I was aware that she had just vomited up blood." Karen started to interrupt when the man held up his hand. "Please, I do not have much time. Let me finish. I can only give you so much information. No, I will not be answering any extra questions. Once I leave this room, you are not to try to find me or contact me. If you see me in public, you must pretend to not know me. I am a stranger after I leave this room."

Clearing his throat, he saw fear start to enter Nicole's face. "I am not here to hurt you or Faith or Hope. Now, where was I? I am the one who knocked the window in and called 911 to come and get Faith out of her car. I was almost too late, and I don't think I will ever forgive myself for that. I believe the extended stress and time in the car may have caused her to pass away more quickly. Be that as it may, I told Faith that I am working on the case and needed as much information as she could give. She handed me her hand-written statement about the chief as well as reports about the other officers she had been collecting information on. When she finished telling me all she knew, she started coughing. There was such pain on her face, I knew it was her time. I told her that her daughter was here in this very hospital and that Faith had already told her about her life. The day you called her to Hope's room, Nicole, and she shared everything, she had actually been speaking to her daughter." Jelissa and Karen immediately looked at Nicole looking for confirmation that the Jane Doe in the adjacent room was, in fact, Hope.

Nicole nodded her head, "It's true, it's Hope. That is why I came in here. I came to get Faith, to bring her to her daughter. I don't understand, what happened?" The man hesitated here, and the tears returned to his eyes once more. "She was extremely happy and so excited, then she started coughing. I turned to get her a glass of water and when I turned back, the coughing had stopped and she was resting her head back against the pillow with a small smile on her face. I thought for a moment that she was just resting while I grabbed her the water. Then, when she didn't move, I came over to wake her, thinking the stress and excitement had exhausted her. She didn't move, though. I realized she was only holding on, so she could know..." here his voice broke, "...so she could know that her daughter was safe."

Wiping fervently at his eyes, he stood up straight, "I am sorry, but I have to go. Her written statement is there on the table. There is also a paper addressed to Hope. I think she knew that she didn't have any more time and was writing her a letter. Please excuse me." Glancing one more time at Faith, the man grabbed his coat and limped out of the room.

Nicole stood from where she had been sitting and walked to the table beside the bed and picked up the letter. Clearing her throat, she began to read it aloud:

My dearest Hope,

I am writing you this letter because I do not think that I have much time left. I have written you a letter every week that you have been gone and then some. Some days, the need to see you was so great that I would just write and write and write. Today is your birthday, sweetheart, and I am so very proud of the woman that you have become. In the safe in my room, there is an envelope deeding everything I have to you. I didn't tell you, but I have slowly been filling a savings account for you to be able to accomplish whatever you set your mind to. Every year on your birthday, I put $1000 in that account, increasing the amount steadily until today, when I added the last amount: $18,000. I am sure you are thinking to yourself, why? If this is my final letter to you, why am I going into this? That's easy. Because you are my daughter and I love you so very much. I need you to know that even though I cannot be here in person for you anymore, I am still here for you. You are my everything. Your very beauty inspires everyone around you to be a better person. You are so gracious and smart and perfect.

I know these last few months have been difficult for you. And I know you may have had to do things that no young lady should ever have to go through. I also know that you are strong. You are going to need people in your life who make you feel that you can lean on them and rely on them and that they will be in your corner. Let me introduce you to your three aunts. First, you have your Aunt Karen. She already loves you. It is possible that I speak about you all the time to her and she would have been crazy if she hadn't immediately fallen in love with you. The other two women, they have been taking care of me the last couple of days. You see, I was placed in the hospital for a few days after a press conference went wrong. I am sure that your three aunts will be more than happy to fill you in. Aunt Nicole and Aunt Jelissa were two of the sweetest, kindest women that I could have asked to care for me. It was through their compassion that they showed me that you could lean on these women as well.

Now, I am sure you are wondering again, Mom, what are you getting at? Why aren't you here with me when I need you most? And, my beautiful girl, I wanted to be there with you so very much and I am so sorry that I cannot be there when you need me most. A couple years ago, I was diagnosed with breast cancer and I have been doing my very best to defeat it. I have been fighting this battle so that I could see you graduate from high school, so that I could

*see you graduate from college, so that I could see you walk
down the aisle and hold your baby for the very first time. As
I am writing this, I have tears streaming down my face
knowing that you will be doing all these things without me
by your side. And I am hoping you can see that these three
women are going to be there for you. I plan to be watching
from above while you accomplish all these things. Please
know that I am so proud of you and I am not upset with you
about the last conversation that we had at all. Remember,
you are perfection and I love you.*

*Now, the last thing, and this is going to confuse you
and worry you and I am sorry for that. There has been a
young man who has been following me for the last couple
of months. I believe that he is trying to find you. I also
believe he may have done things in his past that he is not
happy about. But I also feel that he is going to be there for
you too. I don't know who he is. I don't know his story. I
just know that when he is near, I know that I am safe and I
feel that you will be too. I know he will be the one to find
you and help you get through this. You will know it is him
by the limp he has when he walks and the most piercing
blue eyes you have ever seen.*

*I am tiring now. I love you, my beautiful Hope, and you
are everything and more than I could ever have asked for.*

> *Your proud and happy mom,*
> *Faith*

By the end of the letter, the three women were all in tears.
Grabbing each other's hands and including Faith in their circle,
they bowed their head and cried for the woman who had
touched their lives so irrevocably. With tears streaming down
their faces, they said their final goodbye.

Chapter 7

Hope waited anxiously for the nurse to come back to her room with her mom. As the minutes ticked by, she started to get extremely anxious and very tired. Deciding that it would be okay to fall asleep, as surely they would wake her when they got back to the room, Hope closed her eyes to rest. She ran over and over in her head what she wanted to say to her mom when she got into the room. Starting first and foremost with being sorry for everything that had happened that last day. Thinking about the last words she said, Hope drifted off, determined to recant those words at her first opportunity.

Opening her eyes, she found herself standing back in front of the yellow door. The door had changed to the point where Hope barely recognized it. Where before it had looked shiny and new, it now looked worn. Stress marks, rough wood, cracked and peeling paint, and rusty hinges. The only part of the door left unchanged was the handle of shining brass. She reached for the handle, and expecting to find it warm like she had the last time, she gasped in surprise when she found the metal to be chilled. She pulled back her hand, as the chill from the metal seemed to permeate the air and then her. Shaking off her fear, deeming it unreasonable, she pushed the door open. The same forest was there, beautiful greens and browns. The difference: today it was raining. The rain was coming down in sheets and Hope was immediately soaked through her clothes.

She turned back to go back through the door, only it was no longer there. Deciding that she needed to get to cover as quickly as possible, she ran for the cave. Slipping and sliding the entire way, she was soaked and dirty by the time she got to the cave. Running her hands through her hair to remove some of the water, she started calling out for her mom through the cave. Not seeing her, she decided to sit down next to the pool and clean off some of the dirt and mud that had accumulated on her legs. She felt a sudden chill and what felt like a hand on her shoulder. Smiling, she turned, expecting to see her mom kneeling behind her. However, there was no one there. Frowning, she went back to washing off her feet and legs. Removing her shoes, she sat and dangled her legs at the edge of the pool, shivering slightly at the chill.

As she sat on the edge of the pool, she felt the warmth of her mom's presence. Once again glancing behind her and not seeing her, she realized that she would not be finding her mother in this place ever again, that while her warmth could still be found here, her mom was gone. With that came the realization that her mother was dead. She did not know how she knew this with such certainty, but the minute she did, she was washed in an overwhelming feeling of loss. The shock came first and she realized that she was alone, truly alone. Sitting in complete silence, she felt the last vestiges of hope start to drain from her.

The turmoil she felt within completely defied the cool demeanor she showed on the outside. As she sat staring at the water, she contemplated what it would feel like if she dove into the pool and went to the bottom. She wondered if she would feel pain. She wondered how it would feel to drown. To die in the place where she was last with her mother. The last words she had said to her mother was that she hated her. Now, the last words she wanted to say to herself were the same. "I hate me," she whispered.

The minute the words left her mouth, she felt a warm wind enter the cave. It wrapped itself around her and she felt the warmth of her mother's arms envelope her. She felt strength and compassion. She felt like she was finally home. Then, she felt something different. Something calming and clean. She was struggling to come to terms with what this new feeling was when she felt another new presence next to her. Then, she heard a voice whisper, "Hope."

Startled awake at the sound of her name, Hope gasped in fear waiting for the fist, whip, belt, or foot that would connect next. She knew better than to fall asleep before her time was up. She knew better than to make any sound, for it could mean the difference between a backhand and a whip. Closing her eyes, she sought for solace where she could find it. Realizing that it was now in the cave, she immediately tried to take herself back to the yellow door.

"Hope, sweetheart, it's Nicole. I was just in here with you. I told you I was going to go get your mother. Are you awake?" Nicole looked nervously at Karen and Jelissa when she realized that Hope seemed to be withdrawing into herself.

Suddenly popping open her eyes, Hope made eye contact with Nicole. Looking from her to the other two women in the room, she once again stopped her gaze on Nicole. "She's gone. Isn't she?" she whispered.

Nicole looked askance at having to be the one to deliver the news. She tried to answer Hope when she looked helplessly at Karen and Jelissa. "It's okay. I know she's gone," Hope said calmly. "I know that she loves me and is proud of me. I know this as much as I know that I am going to miss her more than anything." Tears started running down Hope's cheeks, completely unheeded. "I know that she will be with me forever, when I need her most. I know that she has done everything in her power to make sure that I am taken care of. I know that I am…"

What was stopping Hope so suddenly was an emotion, an emotion that had been building up for the last four months. Loss. A word that she knew nothing about four months ago. She knew that her father had left her when she was 7, however, she did not really remember it and had no desire to. This was bone-deep. This felt like her entire world was being ripped apart. Her mom was her strength and her foundation. She needed her like she had never needed anyone else. Body-wracking sobs consumed Hope as she tried to come to terms with never seeing her mother ever again.

Jelissa leaned over and started to pull her into a hug when Hope recoiled from her with immense fear in her eyes. "No! Please do not touch me," she cried out.

Crestfallen, Jelissa pulled away from Hope. She did not know what to do. She started wondering if perhaps Faith was wrong to have said that she would be an aunt to this beautiful, broken girl. Remembering this, Jelissa held the letter silently out to Hope. "It's from your mom. She just finished writing it." Hope took the letter, wincing in pain with the movement.

"May I read this in privacy, please? Also, may I have some pain medicine? I am hurting, and I do not just mean physically. I need to rest and come to terms with never seeing my mom ever again. Never feeling her warm touch. Never having anyone to lean on ever again," said Hope. Nodding, Nicole leaned over and inserted the medicine into her IV. Walking towards the door, she stopped, "Happy Birthday, Hope."

As the door clicked shut, Hope leaned her head back against the pillow on her bed and breathed in deeply. Catching the faint scent of her mom on the letter, she silently told her mother goodbye before pulling open the letter. Reading the letter brought varying emotions; tears being consistent throughout. Realizing that her mom had been hiding the cancer from her brought anger, sorrow, regret, and understanding. She could still see the exhaustion on her mom's face during the last conversation they had shared. Wishing she had known what was going on, she let the anguish wash over her.

Next, she was overcome with such gratitude and awe when she realized what her mom had done for her with the savings account. Lying there, she tried to think of some way she could use that money to make her mom proud, quickly realizing that now was not the time to make that happen. Finally, she was amazed by the description of the man her mom had written, for she recognized him. The man was younger and had visited her in the brothel a couple of times. He had asked her to speak to no one and would simply come in and sit on his e-reader, occasionally grabbing a whip or paddle and snapping it. It was a relief and scary all at the same time as he never actually touched her. Even to remove the chains. He simply sat reading and writing. He never spoke to her, except for the first time when he had come in, and even that had been in soft tones that she had barely understood through the pounding in her head.

Reminiscing about what had happened on those days, she suddenly realized what the nurse—Aunt Nicole, she mused— had said on her way out of the room. Today was her birthday. Hope waited for the emotion to come. Surely she would feel happy, sad, angry, or something. Instead, she felt nothing. Feeling like something was wrong with her, she tried to think of something that would make her sad and force her crying. That did not work. She tried to think of something that made her happy; that did not work either. She was empty of all emotion. She was broken.

Broken was a word that Hope was extremely familiar with. Broken was something she had experienced the first time she had drunk water in captivity. Broken was the first time she had helped a man come to completion to get out of a dark room. Broken was the first time she had felt the back of a hand to her jaw, breaking her lip open and tasting her own blood. Remember the things she had done and all the things she had experienced that broke her started to make her feel ill. Then, she realized that all those other things, they did not break her. She had a glue that was holding her together. Her mom was her glue. Knowing that her mom would always be there, that is what had held her together. Now, without her mom, she experienced what breaking really was.

She could feel her heart rate increase; feel her heart pounding so rapidly in her chest that she felt her breath coming in short gasps. Every breath she took started feeling as though someone was stepping on her chest. She felt knives stab in between her ribs as she tried to regulate her breathing. Suddenly, Hope realized that the walls seemed to be exceptionally close to her. She had not realized before that the room was this small. The hospital gown was far too close to her neck and she could feel it rubbing away there, cutting off her capacity to breathe. Reaching up, Hope started pulling at the gown, needing it to get off her chest. She realized that the more she tried to breathe, the more she could not, and fear started to consume her. Hope realized she had lost feeling in her fingertips, and the fear became even more consuming. Just before she lost consciousness, she thought she saw someone rush into her room. However, by then the yellow door beckoned.

Nicole rushed into the room when she heard the heart monitor beeping. Not understanding what was happening, she thought perhaps the chief had decided to try an attack on Hope next. Then, she quickly dismissed that thought as ludicrous thinking, as the man did not know that Hope was in the hospital. Or did he? That man had known, and she did not even understand how he knew who Hope was before she had. After checking on Hope and seeing that she appeared to be sleeping, she went back to her desk at the nurse's station. Grabbing her book, she decided she would just finish the chapter she had started earlier.

While sitting and reading, she got to thinking how it was possible that a man she had never seen was so quick at determining who both women were. She knew that he said she should not be looking into him, but she was so terribly curious as to why he knew. She had absolutely nothing to go on, then realized that the hospital would have cameras. Considering how she could get security to show her the tapes without giving away too much information, she realized that she was doing the exact opposite of what he had asked and the trust that Faith had put in him. Completely at war with herself, she decided to do everything in her power to make things easier for Hope in whatever way that she could. Realizing that she turned 18 today, Nicole wondered if she should talk to Jelissa and Karen about grabbing Hope some balloons and maybe a cupcake.

Walking over to Faith's room, she peeked her head in to see Jelissa asleep on the couch and Karen asleep in the recliner next to the bed. They would need to take care of Faith soon, but she would let them rest a little longer. Turning to walk out of the room, she bumped into a chair next to the wall, a noise that should have startled them awake. Immediately contrite, she turned to apologize, when she realized that neither woman had moved. Confused, she intentionally made the same noise with the chair, banging it against the wall. When they did not move again, she walked over to Jelissa lying on the couch. She shouted her name and pulled her shoulder to turn her over. When she turned her, Jelissa's eyes were wide open in a glazed stare, completely unseeing, her mouth was open in a scream. Gasping and pulling away, she ran to Karen's side, terrified by what she would find. When she turned the chair to see her face, Nicole screamed in terror when she saw the glazed eyes of Karen staring back at her.

Suddenly, she felt hands on her shoulders and, in fear, she started to scream, knowing that it was her who would be going next.

"Nicole! Wake up!" Jelissa yelled as she shook Nicole's shoulders. "Wake up honey, it's only a dream! You're okay!"

Disoriented and terrified, Nicole opened her eyes to see Jelissa and Karen staring at her with concern etched on their faces. Looking down, she realized that she had fallen asleep at her desk, her book still open. She could not think of a time she had ever fallen asleep while reading and was terrified that maybe she was still dreaming.

"What happened? You screamed and it woke us up. You look terrified," Karen said.

"I had an awful dream, you two, you were…I cannot even say it. Your eyes were open, and I don't think I will ever forget that fear of finding the two of you in that state. You were in Faith's room, I went in to check on you two and thought you were sleeping. Then, when you didn't move, I tried to wake you, only I couldn't wake you up." Karen's hand went to her throat as Nicole was talking.

"What happened?" Karen whispered.

"I don't know, you looked like you had just asphyxiated. Your eyes were wide open and I didn't know what to do. I was terrified that you guys were gone and I would be burying three friends and trying to help Hope." Nicole shook her head as she dropped her chin to her chest, completely overwhelmed by the potential of taking care of a teenager who had been through so much.

"Well, there was one good thing that came out of the dream. The reason that I went looking for you guys was to see if you think we should do anything for Hope's birthday. And Karen, maybe we should send Jelissa to get the balloons," she teased. She hoped that with the teasing she could shake off the fear and chill that were running through her body.

Karen pretended to be affronted, then could not help but start laughing when she remembered the 'It's a Girl' balloon she had brought for Faith. Sobering quickly, she could not believe she had forgotten so soon that Faith was gone. It hurt. There was this spot inside of her that felt so empty without her. "I actually am fairly skilled at making cakes. I can make some cupcakes. I have been considering opening a gourmet shop with cakes and cupcakes and cookies. This will be the perfect opportunity to try out new flavors," Karen started speaking even more rapidly as she started planning her cupcake designs, slowly wandering away to grab her purse and keys from Faith's room as she left.

Laughing, Jelissa started to head out as well to go pick up some clothes and toiletries and balloons for the birthday girl. Wishing she could find the man who was going to be an integral part of Hope's life now to celebrate with them, she jotted down a quick note and grabbed some tape to attach it to Hope's hospital room's door.

Happiness and hope were born this day, not long ago. Gathering together to make it known with the last light of day.

Satisfied that the note was obscure enough that a regular passerby would disregard as a useless fortune but he would recognize what was going on, Jelissa walked down the hall. She wondered if the man had read the letter from Faith to Hope. She did not think he had. Though based on him not saying anything about the relationship she hoped would come, Hope was going to need as much support and as many people as possible to rally behind her. Smiling to herself, she continued to walk down the hallway, not seeing a nurse walk behind her and read the note on the wall. Uncertain of its meaning, she left it there after snapping a quick picture of it and texting it to someone named 'Master.'

Leaving the hospital, Jelissa rushed to get to her car and get shopping done as quickly as possible, hoping that she could take a nap before the party began. She started to step off the curb when she realized she should have said something to Hope and Nicole before she left. Turning quickly, she stepped up on the curb just as a car narrowly missed her, smacking the curb with its tires. Jelissa gasped as she stumbled away from the car. Turning quickly, she tried to see if she could see the person in the front seat, but their tires squealed as they shot out of the parking lot to get away as quickly as possible. Heart racing,

Jelissa turned to run into the hospital when she saw a man peel away from the wall of the hospital and walk towards her.

Jelissa started to tremble when she feared that the man was there to finish the job the person in the car had started, when she noticed the very prominent limp. Sighing in relief, she slowed her pace and then dropped her hands to her knees when the adrenaline left her body. It was then that she realized what Faith had meant about feeling safe and protected when he was near.

"Are you okay?" she heard him whisper to her as he pulled out a cigarette and lit it. Justifying to others his need to stop.

"Yes. I'm okay, thank you," Jelissa whispered, straightening slowly to not draw attention to the two of them.

"I got your note. I will do what I can," he said briskly as he walked away.

Jelissa stared straight ahead and walked back into the hospital, wanting desperately to turn around and ask him not to leave. The minute he walked away, she felt like she was alone again and someone was going to want to hurt her. Seeing an officer in the lobby, she started to walk towards him to report the incident, when she got a pain in her stomach making her feel like it would not be in her best interest to bring the previous matter to his attention. Walking briskly to the nurse's desk, she did not see Nicole there and started to worry. Deciding she would check in on Hope and then try to find Nicole, Jelissa pushed her way into Hope's room just as Nicole was pulling aside the hospital gown on Hope's shoulders to start checking on some of the wounds.

Both women immediately gasped when she entered and Jelissa realized that she had not knocked before entering. "I am so sorry, ladies; my head isn't in the right place without any sleep. I was actually just coming in to see if either of you ladies needed anything from the store before I headed out."

Hope immediately shook her head no and looked away just as her stomach grumbled. She blushed a crimson red upon everyone in the room hearing the sound. Then, as though this was contagious, Jelissa's stomach grumbled as well.

"Well, I guess this answers that question. But now the next question is: tacos, burgers, or pizza?" Nicole asked laughing. "Or better yet, doughnuts!"

Jelissa turned and gave the evil eye to Nicole on the word doughnuts as Hope looked back and forth between the two women. "I do not need anything, thank you," she whispered.

"Perfect," Jelissa said. "That means I get to choose what's for dinner! Oh, this will be fun. I will be back in about an hour or two." Walking out of the room, she saw the note from the door flutter to the ground. Knowing he had seen it, she picked it up and started to throw it away when she saw the other writing on the note.

And tonight, that hope will die.

She hoped that Nicole had not seen this part of the note and hoped even more that the man with the limp had seen it, so that he would be here tonight. Rushing to the vending machine, she grabbed some trail mix and chocolate bars with nuts and then headed back to the room to drop off the snacks. As she walked down the hallway, she saw a man with a limp and got excited that she could show him the note. Except that when his head lifted and she saw his face, she realized that this was not the same man and kept walking. Only now, knowing that there were two men with a limp, she was terrified wondering which man was the man she could trust.

Chapter 8

As he walked away from the building, he knew he was taking a big risk talking to Jelissa Michaels. Single, 32, brown hair, brown eyes, brown skin, five-feet-six, lived at home alone with her cat, and usually ate microwave dinners for meals. She graduated at the top of her class, and no one understood why she had not chosen to be a doctor instead of a nurse. He figured there was a man in there somewhere; he had just not found him yet.

He was not sure what to make of the note he had found on the door of Hope's room. He wondered if it had been Jelissa or Nicole; and now that he had seen Jelissa, he knew it was her. He did not know how he could be involved without blowing his cover, but he knew that he needed to be there. Lately, when he slept, all he seemed to dream about was something yellow. It did not make sense, as he could not remember where he had seen or heard of anything important that was yellow.

Putting out his cigarette and throwing it away, he grimaced at the smell. He did not smoke, but they came in handy when he needed to start a conversation with a lead. Walking quickly away from the building, he climbed into his jeep and headed to the store. Even if he could not make it to the gathering tonight, he still planned to leave something for the captivating woman in that hospital bed. Putting his car into gear, he glanced up one more time at the entrance of the hospital and saw Jelissa rushing out with a piece of paper clutched in her hand. Figuring she had made a list in order see what to pick up for tonight, he smiled softly, enjoying the happiness she seemed to exude around Hope and Nicole.

Starting to back out, he glanced up once more to see a man with a limp walk out behind her. Disregarding him as a patient, he backed the car out of the space and drove to the entrance of the hospital parking lot. Glancing up one last time to the rearview mirror to check his surroundings, he saw the man rush to his car, no limp evident in his stride anymore. He watched as Jelissa exited the parking lot from the employee section and the man following her every move.

Realizing quickly that he would not be having an off night, he pulled out behind the gray sedan that was following behind Jelissa's bright red Volkswagen Beetle.

Watching the car following Jelissa, he decided to try running the plate. When he realized that it was, in fact, a rental car and not something he would be able to pull up any information about, he jotted down the information to look into at a later time. Considering that the person who was following Jelissa was someone who professionally took care of getting rid of someone as a logical possibility, he wanted to take no risks. Wondering about what threat Jelissa could possibly pose to anyone having anything to do with the sex trafficking ring, he continued to follow until she pulled into a parking lot of a store with a popular red circle for a logo. He discreetly parked two aisles over and hopped out of his car, preparing to go into the store. He saw Jelissa get out as well and head straight in, seemingly oblivious to everything going on around her. When she dropped a quarter on the ground and bent down to pick it up, he realized that she was not nearly as oblivious as she had seemed.

As the man who had been following her, no longer with a limp, started to pass by her, she stood up suddenly and ran into him.

"I am so sorry! I did not see you standing there. Clumsy me! How could I have been so rude? Please, let me buy you a coffee or something to make it up to you." Batting eyelashes, she flirted with the man and placed her hand on his shoulder. The man seemed bewildered at the woman flirting with him and seemed unsure about how to respond to the blatant 'come hither' look in her eyes.

While watching the exchange, Jelissa glanced over her shoulder, catching his eye and smiled determinedly. *What is she doing?* he thought to himself.

Why would she be giving this man this attention? It is almost like she is providing a distraction. He watched as she escorted him into the store and walked over to the café, ordering herself a coffee and a scone. The man, still befuddled at what was happening, ordered himself the same thing she had and then proceeded to pay for the order when Jelissa said that she had left her purse in the car. Realizing that Jelissa was giving him the perfect distraction, he went back out to the parking lot. Suddenly, he saw the lights flash on in Jelissa's car. Walking over to it, he realized that she had, in fact, left her purse in the car. Then, he saw the note on her front seat:

I have no idea who the man that is following me is. But, if I am honest, I don't know you either. Faith said that she felt safe with you. So I am going to trust her judgment. I am going to distract him. Do what you need to figure out who he is.

Impressed and pleased that she was so clever, he quickly walked over to the other man's car. Checking the door, he was not surprised when he found the door locked. There was nothing in the car that would show him who this person was or if he were friend or foe. He started to wander back into the store, deciding he would shop while keeping an eye on her, when he decided that he could not, in good conscience, leave her purse in the car. Grabbing it and then locking up the car, he started to once more head into the store. Seeing her in the café, he coughed slightly. She glanced up at the cough and started chuckling. Placing her hand on the man's hand across the table and squeezing it, she excused herself.

"Um, excuse me, sir. That is my purse. Please tell me I did not leave it on the top of my car again. I am forever doing that!" Jelissa exclaimed.

"You did, ma'am. I hope you don't mind that I brought it in with me. I couldn't leave it out there." Smiling as he spoke, he quickly asked under his breath if she was okay.

"You are too sweet! Thank you so much, sugar!" she smiled and nodded before heading back to her table with the purse strap over her shoulder. Momentarily confused, he stood there for a minute before making his way to get a cart. He clearly could not stand there and watch them. Grabbing a cart, he immediately went to the women's section trying to find something for the gathering that night. Not finding anything, he went to the jewelry section and realized that this would be way overboard. Not sure what his role would even be and why he was invited, he started to leave, figuring he would buy her a gift card or something. As he turned, something yellow caught his eye. Turning back around, he saw a beautiful yellow scarf made of soft silk. Being inexplicably drawn to it, he tossed it in his cart. Feeling like a fool, he left that department and went shopping for what he actually needed. He hoped he would see Jelissa as soon as possible to determine if she was okay.

Jelissa dropped the quarter on the ground asking herself what she was doing and wondering if this would even work. This man could be following her to kill her. At least she had seen the blue jeep pull out and knew that Blue Eyes was close. That was what she was going to call him until he could introduce himself properly. Seeing the shoe of the man who had followed her since the hospital next to her, she stood and bumped into him, hoping it was not obvious what she was doing.

Apologizing, she led him inside, hoping that Blue Eyes would figure out what she was doing. When she caught his eye, she made sure he heard about her purse. When he left the store, she was terrified that it had not worked. Now, she was completely alone and she was going to need to do this all by herself.

Sitting at the table, she found herself commanding 100% of the man's attention. Something that had not happened to her in over five years. Pain crossed her features as she realized that she was missing this special something that could not ever be hers again. The man in front of her caught the look and inquired what could possibly be wrong with her.

"Oh, the coffee is just a little warmer than I was anticipating. I have this great distraction in front of me," she cooed.

"Well, thank you. I am happy to be a distraction, though I am not sure I like that my kind of distraction caused you pain," he responded.

"Where are my manners? My name is…"

"Jelissa Michaels. I know. And I also know that the reason you dropped that money and bumped into me was so that the man who followed us from the hospital would be able to go check out my car and see who I am," he interrupted. Fear flashed in Jelissa's eyes when she realized that she had not been as subtle as she had hoped. "I have no intention of hurting you, Jelissa. Though if I am honest, I wonder if I may anyway."

Jelissa swallowed, trying to compose herself as she listened to what he was saying. She beeped her car hoping Blue Eyes was by there and hoped it would speed his time back to her. Waiting 30 seconds, she beeped it again as she took a bite of her scone. She felt there was no need for pretense anymore, because he had just made it clear that he knew what she was doing. Now the issue arose about how she would make her escape.

"So, if you have no intention of hurting me, why are you following me?" Jelissa queried, then wondered why she was poking the bear. She should have left it alone rather than making the situation worse. Glancing up, she saw Blue Eyes come back into the store and cough. Relief flashed in her eyes as she glanced up and caught him looking at her.

"Before I answer that question, why don't you go over there, get the purse you conveniently left in your car, and tell him you are doing just fine and no longer need his help? Make it convincing," he quietly demanded.

Smiling quickly to cover her fear, she grasped his hand and squeezed as she left the table, digging her thumbnail into his hand as deep as possible when she left. When the grip was not returned, she hastened to Blue Eyes' side. After reassuring him that all was well, she made her way back to the table.

"What is it that you want from me?" she asked as she sat back down.

"That is something even I have not decided."

"That doesn't make any sense. You obviously want something from me, otherwise you wouldn't have been following me. So, spit it out. I have stuff I have to do tonight," Jelissa snapped.

"Wow, you have quite the temper when riled. I like it when my women fight back," he said snidely.

Jelissa felt extremely ill but knew she had to keep her wits about her. She decided that if this was going to be her last foray into the shopping world, she would go all out. Standing up, she felt a hand grip her arm. Looking down, she saw what she thought was a flash of panic and concern that was immediately covered by anger. Sure she was imagining things, she tried to pull her hand loose. "Let go of me. I haven't given you permission to touch me. And, no, this is not one of those times when no means yes."

Standing with her instead, he kept his grip on her hand and started walking with her towards the door. At the last minute, she grabbed a cart and made like she was going to go shopping. "You will let go of me or you will let me shop. Your choice. But you are asking for a scene if you do not let me do what I want." She stated mustering up as much courage as she could. Grabbing the cart, he started to push.

"I just wanted to be able to push the cart for you, pet," he replied.

"I am not your pet and you would do well to not address me as such," Jelissa responded fiercely. Confused, she felt a quick pull of desire at being called pet. She did not understand. This man was clearly here to hurt her. So why would she feel that? Especially after what he had said about women fighting back. Gasping suddenly, she realized why this man seemed familiar. He was the man she had seen leaving Hope's room the night before. She had thought it was Blue Eyes, except he was sitting in the waiting room and had already left when she saw the man with the limp. "Wait a second. You aren't limping," she accused.

His face registered surprise as he quickly tried to cover up his blunder, "It is because I am holding onto the cart. It helps."

"No, you don't walk with a limp naturally. I would know, I am a nurse after all."

"Well, that was a snide comment that I was not expecting from you. Interesting that you feel it necessary to say something to try and put yourself above others. I wasn't expecting it from you. It surprises and disappoints me," he said softly.

Jelissa felt the sting of disappointment; a feeling she had not felt since long ago. Confused by her response to this man, she decided to treat it as though he had not been following her and had not threatened her. "Well, you know my name, what is yours?"

He glanced sideways at Jelissa, trying to determine what name to give her. "Let's go with Henry," he replied slowly.

"Well, Henry, and, no, I don't think that is actually your name, what is your last name?"

"Actually, pet, my name is Henry. No, I am not willing or able to tell you my last name." Glancing up sharply, he suddenly whispered, "I need you to do your best to look frightened."

Completely flabbergasted, Jelissa started to look at him incredulously, when his fingers started digging into her arm.

"I will kill you if you don't do everything I say. Please do not let my charm convince you otherwise," he stated fiercely.

Jelissa was so overcome with fear that she started to feel extremely nauseous. She did not understand what was happening and why he seemed to be so bipolar. He was right, though. She, most definitely, was being sucked in by the charm, and she would never make the mistake again of trusting that he was there to do anything other than hurt her. "I truly did plan to shop. Is there any point?" She sniffled as she said this. It was becoming increasingly obvious to her that she would not be making it to the party tonight. She was so scared for herself and so sad that she would be disappointing Hope. She thought about Mr. Tickles, her cat at home, and realized that she did not have anyone who would be able to care for him. No one would even think to check on him. Overcome with emotion, Jelissa felt a sob well up in her.

Henry tensed as the first sob escaped and his grip immediately loosened on her arm. He had a role to play, though, and he would follow through with it. Seeing a sales associate approach, he realized that collateral damage might occur.

"Um, ma'am, is everything all right?" the pimple-faced teenager asked.

Before Henry could respond, Jelissa did. "Oh, my goodness, yes, my boyfriend here, he just told me he loved me for the very first time. He hates that I am a crier when I am happy. It absolutely throws him for a loop." Reaching up, she patted him on the cheek. The message clearly conveyed was that she would do what she had to, even if she was scared and worried. Smiling awkwardly, the teenager walked away.

"You lied very easily there," Henry said, with disgust evident in his tone.

"Don't be an asshole. None of this is easy. You are literally holding me against my will. Answer the question, Henry. Is there even any point in my shopping?" her voice trembled.

"No," he replied simply.

Almost collapsing, Jelissa decided to give up any pretense of being happy and decided to take her chances. As she tensed to scream, she heard Henry whisper, "Please don't." Certain that she had misheard him, she caught his eye. That was when she saw the tension in his body.

"We are being watched, aren't we? And it isn't by the man who brought me my purse, is it?" Jelissa queried softly.

Deciding it was better that she knew, he simply turned his head and, staring her in the eye, replied, "Yes, my pet."

Suddenly realizing that he had not checked on Jelissa, Blue Eyes made his way to the front of the store. It did not take long to see that he had a man following him. Acting nonchalant, he stopped to peruse the DVDs on the front lanes. Seeing one he thought Hope might like, he picked it up. Unsure why he was inexplicably drawn to comedy rather than romance, he tossed it into his cart. The man trailing him went up to a lane, then did a great job of pretending he had something to buy. Going over to the cards section, suddenly Blue Eyes realized that he needed one of those too. *Oh, well*, he thought to himself. Walking over to the cards, he found a very generic 'Happy Birthday' card. This one with a garden scene on front with yellow chairs.

There I go again, gravitating towards something that is so out of character for me. Behind him, he heard what sounded like a muffled sob. Turning, he saw a sales associate asking a woman if she was okay, when he realized that it was Jelissa. Unable to hear her answer, seeing her pat the other man's face, he was not sure how he should respond. He continued to look through cards when he glanced up in time to see fear wash over Jelissa's face. Concerned, he started paying a little more attention to what people were around him. One man, a man who seemed familiar, did not even seem to be trying to blend in. He simply watched the 'couple' in the middle of the aisle. There was also nothing in Jelissa's cart, though he was certain she had come here for Hope. Not sure if he should attempt a rescue, he was dumbfounded when he watched Jelissa drop her head to the man's chest. When his arm flinched as though to return the gesture, Blue Eyes was even more disconcerted. Wondering if he had misread Jelissa or perhaps the other man, he decided to push it further than he should.

Pulling out his cell phone, he started to once again head towards the cash registers, texting away. He crashed into Jelissa and the other man's cart. He watched as his 'tail' and the other man's 'tail' did too. Realizing this other man was not on the side of the other men following him, he wondered who this other player was to the game. "Pardon me. This cell phone is constantly getting me in trouble. Ma'am, did I hurt you at all?"

Jelissa looked at Blue Eyes with tears still swimming in her eyes. "He knows you know me. It's okay." Henry tensed beside her, angry that she had not followed his directions. He had not determined if this man opposite him was someone whom he could trust yet, and he did not like that his cover had essentially been blown.

Making a split-second decision, "Hey Derek! Is that you? Oh man, it has been so long since I have seen you! I am sure you don't remember me. Henry from…"

"Oh, yah! Oasis Glen High School! You were friends with my older brother!" Blue eyes, now Derek, answered.

"Yes, exactly," Henry replied. Placing his arm around Jelissa's waist, he said, "Have you met my girlfriend Jelissa?"

"I have, actually, she was a nurse who helped me when I injured my leg a few months back playing soccer. Tore my ACL," Derek responded.

Henry's arm tensed around Jelissa's waist. He did not like the idea that she had helped this other man and wondered if it was fabricated for the cover of the tails or if it was true. Glancing at Jelissa, he was surprised to see the mirth in her eyes. Suddenly, she started giggling. "Oh, my goodness, I remember you! You…" overcome with giggles, she could not continue. Henry looked from her to the other man, not certain how to respond. Smiling softly, he inquired what had happened.

"I think she is laughing about the time I may have called her extremely attractive when I was very drugged after my surgery. I personally have no recollection of this, but she and the other nurses reminded me incessantly while I was there." Shaking his head, Derek motioned to the cart. "Are you guys having trouble finding what you're looking for? I practically live at this store, I can help you guys find what you're looking for, then maybe we can grab a coffee."

Jelissa quickly interjected, grateful for the lifeline. "Oh, my goodness, that would be so great. I usually don't shop here, if I am honest."

"Well, sounds like my pet has decided. Let's get the shopping done quickly, I need to get back to work in about 30 minutes." Turning around, Henry started pushing the cart towards the women's section. He was momentarily stunned when Jelissa wrapped her arm with his, then leaned up and kissed him on the cheek. The trio walked on to the women's section while the two tails made eye contact. The one looking at the cards, tossed the card in his cart and nodded his head towards the front door. Abandoning the cart and all semblance of blending in, they headed to the front door and left.

Seeing this, Henry and Derek stopped and looked at each other. "Friend or foe?" Henry asked.

"To Jelissa, friend. To you, I do not know you. I also do not like you, because you made her cry. However, I also get the feeling that although you came here with the intention of hurting her, you have realized that this is not in your best interest. So, I would say let's keep up the ruse in case there is another tail and we will sort this out later. Jelissa will need to show up at the gathering she is shopping for tonight, or I will hunt you down and kill you. Is that understood?" There was no prevarication in his tone. Henry was taken aback by this, wondering at their relationship.

"Jelissa has already been informed that she will not be going to the gathering tonight. Unfortunately, I am going to have to take her with me when I leave here," Henry replied firmly.

"He did tell me that. I don't understand it at all, though. Also, speaking of the gathering, Derek, I wanted to show you that someone else wrote a note on the bottom of the message that I left for you. Here it is in my purse." Handing him the note, she once again leaned into Henry. Watching their exchanges, Derek noticed that not once had they stopped touching since he had seen them sitting at the table in the café. Glancing down at the note, he realized that his option for sitting out of the gathering tonight had just been taken out of his hands. Unsure why, he handed the note over to Henry.

"Damn," Henry sighed. "Guess that takes that option right out of my hands. We will be going to this gathering tonight." Glancing sharply at the man by his side when he chuckled, he cocked his head and looked questioningly at him.

"I was literally just thinking the exact same thing. I cannot believe I am doing this. My name is Joe. I am an undercover agent for an organization that is strictly off the books. I am breaking protocol by telling you this. I know you named me Derek, but I will not answer to it." Holding out his hand to Henry, he wondered what Henry would do. He had just laid all his cards on the table.

"My name is Henry, I have a feeling you and I are not even aware that we work for the same organization, as mine is off the books as well." Hearing a sound next to him, he turned to look at Jelissa. "Yes, pet, my name really is Henry."

"Can we shop now? This is all too much. I have only slept a couple hours in the last two days. I need to get clothes for Hope and a present," said Jelissa. With that, the trio waded into the women's section pulling out clothes for Hope. To any onlooker, they looked like a trio of friends who had gone shopping and happened to meet up. When, in fact, Jelissa was terrified out of her mind. She did not know why she was having

70

the reactions to Henry that she was. She had not felt this way for almost six years.

Henry was regretting lying in front of his pet. He wanted her to trust him. He most definitely did not work for any organization that was off the books. Joe was watching the other shoppers like a hawk, realizing that they had missed a tail. Only this one he recognized. A bald man with quite the paunch.

Chapter 9

Nicole was starting to get worried. It was almost 7 and both Karen and Jelissa were not back. Considering whether or not she should go out and grab a few things, she realized that she would not be able to leave Hope for that long without leaving her terrified.

Nicole was also a little peeved that they had left, thereby making it her responsibility to take care of Faith. She had taken care of preparing the body to the best of her ability and then asked Hope if she would like to see her mom one last time. She was not surprised when Hope declined. Hope wanted to remember her mom how she was before the illness had ravaged her body. She also had been tied to a chair and forced to watch every time her mom was on the screen. So she had watched the changes in her mom. The woman at the brothel had hoped it would break her spirit seeing her mom and knowing that her mom could not find her. However, hearing Faith's voice had, instead, soothed her and gave her strength. Many of the other girls had started to resent their parents' inability to find them.

Nicole was so pleased that Hope had opened up to her, but when she had left the room to continue looking after her other patients, Hope had gone back to staring into nothingness. Hoping she could find a way to perk her up, including the birthday gathering tonight, she started to focus on the other patients.

It was past 7 o'clock when Nicole realized that the sun was going down and the other two ladies were not back. She realized that she would be the only one who would be able to take care of Hope. Worry etched her brow as she headed back to Hope's room with a couple of juice boxes and jello from the hospital food cart.

Walking in, she was terrified when she saw two men in her room. They were closing the blinds to the outside of the room to see outside it. Hope was lying on the bed with her eyes closed.

Terrified, she opened her mouth to scream as the door behind her opened and knocked her in the back. Turning quickly to see who was there, she gasped when she saw Jelissa standing behind her. Her gasp alerted the two men in the room to her presence and they turned to see who was there. Both men had their hands go to their waist. Seeing Nicole, they immediately relaxed. Henry made eye contact with Jelissa and chuckled as she brought gift bags into the room in a laundry cart. Slightly chuckling, Jelissa started tossing streamers and balloons at the men.

"Think fast!" she stage-whispered as she threw the balloons at Henry. Only it was clear that she was aiming for his face. He caught the bag and squinted his eyes at her as she smiled mischievously. Nicole watched the interaction, completely confused.

"Okay, time out. What the hell is going on here?" she asked fiercely.

Upon her words, Hope, who had been sleeping in her cave, woke quickly with terror etched on her face.

"I'm sorry, I will not fall asleep again. I am ready for the next client," Hope whispered.

Joe, Henry, Jelissa, and Nicole turned to look at Hope. Nicole blushed crimson red as she realized she had woken Hope from her slumber. "Oh, sweetheart, I am so sorry. I didn't mean to wake you. You are safe, it's Nicole."

"Aunt Nicole…" Hope said in a whisper. Not hearing her, Jelissa and Nicole looked back and forth at each other. A small smile crossed Hope's lips. Seeing this, they all smiled along with her. "I said, Aunt Nicole. If you are going to be my aunt, then be my aunt. Otherwise, I can call you Nicole and we can leave it alone." Turning to Jelissa, "And you are Aunt Jelissa, same thing. Either be the aunt mom requested or do not, but make your decision and stick with it." She then seemed like she was looking for someone when she turned around and saw the men standing behind her. Glancing from one to the next, she gasped in fear.

Karen walked through the doors just as Hope was recoiling from the men in the room, and Karen immediately sprang into action. Grabbing one of the cupcakes off her tray, she threw a cupcake at Joe's face.

"No, wait!" Jelissa started laughing. Joe reached up and wiped frosting and cake off his face. Slowly, he licked his lips, surprise lighting up his face.

"Wow, this is exceptionally good frosting. Thank you, Karen. Nice arm by the way. Next time, aim a little more to the left. Henry has a better catch than I do, clearly." Walking calmly to the sink, he started to wash his hands when he decided to lick a few of his fingers first instead. Suddenly, there was a knock on the door. Turning quickly with his hand going to his hip, he saw Henry do the same.

"Pizza delivery, for a...Nurse Jelissa," the voice on the other side of the door said.

Jelissa started to head to open the door when Henry reached forward and grabbed her arm. Shaking his head subtly, she dipped her head in acknowledgment and turned away to get back to decorating the room. Hope watched all this happen and started to feel like someone was stepping on her chest. Behind her, Joe was washing his hands when he heard the door close and the sound of the monitor start to go off. Hope's heart rate was increasing rapidly. All three of the women leapt forward to check on her. When Hope recoiled, they all looked at each other askance. Drying his hands quickly, he walked directly over to the bed. Sitting down on the side of it, Hope looked up in terror until she saw his face.

"Look at me," he said softly. Hope reached up her hand and placed it on Joe's cheek. When she determined he was real, she withdrew her hand, then whipped it back and smacked him in the face. Joe sat and took the hit. When Hope saw the imprint of her hand start to show on Joe's face, she glanced from her hand down to her bed. "Can you guys give us the room really quick, please," Joe said without turning away from Hope. The room had gone silent at the sound of her hand connecting with Joe's face. With Joe's request, the women looked to each other before Jelissa spoke up.

"Hope," Jelissa started. "Are you okay if we step out for a minute? We still have some more things to grab anyway."

Hope had lifted her head at the sound of Joe's voice asking they leave. Looking furtively into his eyes, she turned and nodded to Jelissa. "Yes, Aunt Jelissa. I think I will be okay. He will not hurt me." Jelissa turned and looked at Henry. He nodded once and they started to exit the room. Nicole and Karen following their lead. Nicole glanced back one more time and saw that Joe had still not moved. Anxious, she stepped out into the hallway and stood there, unwilling to leave the hall in case Hope called for her. She watched as the other two women and Henry left. She turned to look for a chair, when, out of the corner of her eye, she saw Henry reach for Jelissa's hand as they reached the entrance. Jelissa tried to remove her hand, but his grip only tightened. Confused and concerned by this, Nicole sat down to wait.

"I am sorry that I hit you," Hope whispered softly to Joe.

Reaching over, Joe took Hope's hand in his, she flinched and attempted to pull away when he squeezed it gently and let go. "You have nothing to apologize for. I am sure you have a lot of questions and you want to know what is going on. Let me tell you what I can say, and then maybe one day I can tell you everything else," Joe started to get up when Hope laid her hand on his arm.

"Please, stay," she pleaded.

"I was only going to grab a chair and pull it up beside the bed. Or do you want me to stay seated here?" Joe looked perplexed yet patient.

Looking embarrassed, Hope did not answer immediately. "May I ask you a question?" she asked. At his nod, she continued. "Do you walk with a limp?" At the question, Joe looked affronted and sat up straighter before nodding his head imperceptibly.

"Why would you ask me something like that?" Joe snarled.

Hope immediately grimaced and tried to back away from Joe. Scared and confused at his anger, she grabbed her mother's letter from beneath her pillow and wordlessly handed it to him. Joe took the letter and proceeded to read it. When he got to the part about him, his eyes widened in surprise. Looking up at Hope, he responded with awe, "Yes, that is me. I do walk with a limp. ACL surgery. Hoping I won't limp for much longer. My name is Joe, by the way.

"Let me first start by saying that I am so terribly sorry for the times I visited you in captivity and didn't free you. It was one of the hardest things that I have ever done. It was the only way I could find to give you a reprieve. I know you are probably wondering why I didn't get you out and all I can say is that there was more to it than that. There are multiple girls being held there." Clearing his throat, he did his best to continue when he looked up to meet Hope's gaze; she looked completely shell-shocked. "Hope?"

"That was you? I thought maybe it was just my mind playing tricks on me. You would come in and read or write. Just sit there. You would not even look at me. It was like you were disgusted by me. I do not know what was worse. Your looks of disgust or the looks of lust from the other clients." Hope shuddered as she thought of the red door. "May I ask you a seemingly inconsequential question?"

Joe chuckled at her question. He was not expecting such intelligence to come out of someone so young. She was just a kid. Or so he had to keep reminding himself. Glancing once more at Hope, he saw hurt enter her eyes and then harden. He opened his mouth to speak, when she held up her hand. It reminded him of her mother.

"Never mind. I did not mean to inconvenience you with the question." Raising her voice a bit, she called out to Nicole, "Aunt Nicole, will you come back in here please?"

"That is not what I was trying to do. I'm s..."

Nicole came into the room and looked from Joe to Hope. "I did not realize you knew I was waiting outside the door. Is everything okay, sweetheart?" she inquired. She did not see anything untoward happening. However, she presumed Hope would not have called for her if something were not wrong.

"Yes, I am fine. I knew you would not go too far. Thank you for inquiring after my health. I merely have found that Joe and I have nothing else to discuss that should require privacy. I presume, based on the beginnings of decorations and the cupcakes that you all have decided to celebrate my birthday." Upon the completion of Hope's sentence, Jelissa, Henry, and Karen all walked back into the room. Uncertain about how to take her statement, they all looked from one to the other. However, Joe stood and went back to the decorations.

Turning back to Hope with a blank expression, he asked, "What's it gonna be, Hope? Make a decision." Pain crossed Hope's face before she could mask it. Not understanding why he could not seem to say the right thing, he huffed and left the room. He still needed to grab her scarf and the movie from the car anyway. Leaving the room without a word, Hope and the rest watched him go.

Nicole turned to go after him when Hope halted her progress. "No. If he does not want to be here, let him go."

The group started getting back to the festivities. Decorating and laughing and talking. Hope did her very best to have a jovial time. However, she was struggling knowing that she was supposed to be celebrating on the same day that her mother died. I mean, sure she would want her to be happy. Closing her eyes and shaking her head, she missed the door being opened. She dropped her head just as the barrel of a gun came into view. A single shot rang out into the room, quickly followed by a second. Blood spread out across the front of Hope and she fell back against the pillow. Nicole and Jelissa rushed forward as Henry charged the door, chaos reigning supreme through the room.

Chapter 10
Two Weeks Later

Joe stood beside a tree in the cemetery, the dual ceremony for Hope and Faith breaking him further than he thought possible. He could see Jelissa, Karen, and Nicole standing around the caskets as they were lowered into the ground. Henry had disappeared the night of the shooting. Joe had heard the shot ring out in the hallways as he came back into the hospital. His heart dropped to his stomach when he realized he had not been there to protect her. The three women looked so alone standing there. Faith and Hope had not been in the area long enough for more people to attend the service.

Joe suddenly noticed a man loping across the lawn with determined strides. He was heading straight for the women. As he got closer, he saw Jelissa stand up straighter. The man turned his head to check his surroundings and Joe saw his face. It was Henry. A man who definitely did not work for the same organization as Joe. As he neared Jelissa, he spread his arms to reach out and pull Jelissa into his embrace when she shoved him back from her. Fists pounding on his chest until he wrapped her in his arms and sobs wracked her body. Nicole and Karen watched before linking to each other, hands around the other's waist as they watched Jelissa come apart in his arms.

Joe turned to walk away when he heard his name get called by Nicole. Turning back to look at her, he shook his head no and walked away. He could not face the condemnation he knew he would see on their faces.

Nicole watched Joe walk away, the ache she felt was so deep she did not think she would ever be able to heal from it. Feeling Karen squeeze her waist, she laid her head down on her shoulder. The sobs coming out of Jelissa tearing her up inside. That night would forever be etched in their minds. Every time she closed her eyes, she saw the shock come over Hope's face when the bullet struck her. Henry whipping out his gun and firing, the bulling catching the woman in her chest and killing her before she hit the ground. She was amazed when she recognized the night nurse. Though she did not understand her motive for shooting Hope, Jelissa was the one who recognized her as the nurse who was trying to take Faith to see the chief of police the prior day. It was through her getting caught that they did an autopsy on Faith and found that she had been killed. She did not simply die in her sleep as they originally thought.

It was in trying to figure out why this nurse would want to kill Hope and Faith that she started developing anger towards those around her. To find out that Jelissa had received a warning that Hope's killing would happen and had not bothered telling her was infuriating. She could have prevented it. She would have done something to make sure that Hope was safe and did not have to be killed right in front of them. She grew angry at Henry because he did not stop the shooter fast enough. If he would have been paying attention rather than trying to catch Jelissa's eye, then maybe Hope would still be here!

For Henry to show back up now was just wrong and rubbing it in their faces that he really did not care about anything other than Jelissa and the relationship he could cultivate with her. Karen was even worse. Nicole was surprised that she had even shown up at the funeral. She had left that night saying that she needed to get home to her family. She needed to go hug her children. All of these things and nobody even talking about the teenage girl who had gone missing the night before. Everyone knew that she was going to be found in that ring too. Nicole was going to do everything in her power to make sure that she helped find the ring and stopped it. She had hoped to be able to rely on Joe, like Faith had recommended. Clearly that was not going to be an option.

Every day since she had watched the heart monitor flat-line on Hope, she had researched different ways through which she could make a difference. She started showing up to work late, unable to walk down the hallway where she had seen Hope get rushed to her room. She could not go into the room where Faith died or the room where Hope died. Her coworkers and supervisors said that she got too close to the patients and it was unprofessional. Just this morning, she had been suspended, pending review. She walked out saying she quit. Now, she needed to find something else that she could do that would make a difference for those around her. Hopefully without falling in love and losing two of the most important people in her life.

She was still flabbergasted that she had been so affected by these two women this quickly. How was it possible that in less than 48 hours she had welcomed them into her family and then lost them? She had no idea what to do. Everything hurt. Everywhere she looked, she saw a reminder of the women who could have been so much more. And everywhere she looked, she saw one more person who had become a part of this ring. Extricating herself from Karen's arm and throwing a last look of disgust at Jelissa and Henry, Nicole briskly walked to her car. The sudden pain to the back of her head knocking her to the ground unexpectedly. The last thing she saw before her eyes closed was Karen being awkwardly drawn into a hug with Henry and Jelissa.

Karen hated standing next to the women who were supposed to have been aunts for beautiful Hope. The closed casket was a testament to the amount of damage that had been done to Hope. No one was allowed to see her. Karen just wanted to see her beautiful face one last time. Faith had listed her in the will as a guardian. It was her choice to allow Hope to become a donor. Sitting in the meeting with them asking her questions had nearly destroyed her. Every night she went home and hugged her children tighter than she ever had before. Remembering them asking her if they could have her hair and eyes, Karen felt extremely ill. Watching Henry walk across the lawn towards them, she felt herself stiffen. She could tell he was hiding something from them. The fact that he had disappeared for the last two weeks only proved that her thoughts were true. Upon whispering Jelissa's name, Jelissa looked up and met her eyes. Karen inclined her head to Henry.

Seeing the pain come over Jelissa's face, she realized how much damage had been done to all of them. Nicole was keeping herself separate and Karen felt like she could not reel her back in. They had been thrust together by Faith. Obviously Faith had known what she was asking when she pushed the three together. Of course Karen had known Faith the longest and knew that she seemed to have a sixth sense for knowing when people would be good together. When Henry reached them and Jelissa started to hit his chest, Karen felt her chest tighten and the tears she had managed to keep back were finally let loose and fell down her cheeks. Watching Jelissa get enveloped into Henry's arms, she slipped her arm around Nicole, trying to give comfort where she could. Karen was not surprised when she felt Nicole stiffen. She could feel her pull away emotionally, but not physically. Karen felt hope flare back to life inside of her, realizing that maybe there was a way they could come back together. She was startled out of her musings when Nicole suddenly shouted Joe's name. Turning to watch, Joe took a step forward to come to them, then, shaking his head, he walked away. The loss and betrayal she had felt started to melt away when she realized how responsible he probably felt.

When Nicole stiffened in response and walked away, Karen wrapped her arms around her own waist, feeling so alone in this. She was not the glue. Faith and Hope were. So, for them to both be gone, she realized that maybe she would not be able to hold this group together anymore. Suddenly, arms came around her and she stiffened when she felt Henry's touch. Something was off with this man, and she was going to find out what it was. Turning her head to search for Nicole one last time, she saw a black SUV pull away from the curb. No sign of Nicole.

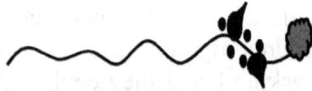

Jelissa stared down at the grave; seeing the caskets getting lowered and knowing who was in them was killing her. She felt so separate from the women standing to her left. Dropping her head to her chest, she tried to rein in the tears that were forever falling down her face. She felt weak and used. That night she had watched as Henry pulled his gun too late. The shot ringing out too long after the first. Initially, he had shoved her into the bathroom attached to the room. After realizing that it was clear, he had pushed her from the room. Seeing the blood on Hope's chest and hearing the doctor call for paddles had nearly broken her.

Sitting in the hallway for almost an hour, she was hopeful that they could bring her back. Henry had walked out of the room trailing a nurse who was pushing Hope on a gurney. Then, looking at her, he said he was sorry and then left the hospital. He just left without a backward glance or anything. She had not seen him since and she did not want to. When she heard her name whispered and she glanced up to see him, she thought for sure that it was a mirage. When he opened his arms, she wanted to go into them so badly. She wanted to find solace and comfort in his arms, but the anger at being abandoned flooded her.

She did not even realize she was pounding his chest with her fists until she felt her own fists next to her cheeks as her forehead pressed to his chest. His arms were like bands of steel around her back. Her hands were tingling and red as they lay against his chest. Feeling his cheek brush against her hair, she was stunned into silence. Then his lips brushed her temple. Jelissa attempted to lean back so she could look at his face, when she heard him whisper, "Not yet."

She collapsed back into him, desperate to believe that he would truly be there for her this time. She was inexplicably drawn to him. She did not know why, but she knew she needed to find out. She felt him squeeze her one last time. His arm started to release from around her. Staggered by the loss of his arm dropping away, she looked up to see why he was pulling away, when she saw him reach out his arm to Karen. Stiffening, she realized he was only hugging them because of their loss. There was nothing special between them. She needed to get over herself and move on. Opening her arm, she pulled a very stiff Karen into their hug. Resigned, she reined her emotions back in.

Chapter 11

The chill coursing through her body felt as though it would never go away. Pain seemed to radiate from every point in her body. Trying to open her eyes, she grimaced in pain. Realizing there was no light, she grasped around trying to remember where she was. The last thing she remembered was pain being blasted into her and then nothing, until now. She could tell she was on the ground but could not discern where. Everything was foggy in her mind while she tried to figure out where she was and why she was there. The pain she felt seemed to radiate from everywhere and nowhere, all at the same time.

"Someone please help me," she gasped.

Joe felt as though he had failed. Every direction he looked in his past, all he could see were opportunities where he had every chance to succeed and instead failed. Even in his sleep, he was haunted by the failures. Every morning when he woke, the first thing he saw on his bedside table was a yellow scarf. The scarf he had left in his car when he went to the birthday party.

He had read the note and knew there was a chance there would be an attempt on Hope's life. Instead of being there for her, he had instead let his anger and something else he had not recognized that night get in his way. Jealousy. He did not recognize it that night and did not understand it now. What had he done? He could still see the hurt and betrayal cross her face when he had chuckled.

Was it his limp? Had it insulted her so much? She could not know of his failures. Was it because he had left her in that room chained? He had not thought her disgusting in the least. Quite the opposite, which made him disgusted with himself. He was a 23-year-old man who was looking at a then 17-year-old and seeing somebody attractive. It was not the make-up, the corsets, or the provocative way she was placed. It was the keenness in her eyes. It was the determination to not show fear. It was the intelligence she had exuded on her birthday. Anger started to surface that he had been unable to help her and seemed to be getting stalled at trying to get into the brothel. Gripping his hands into fists, he stalked back to his car after watching the women beside the grave. Climbing into his blue jeep, he peeled away from the curb, leaving rubber embedded in the road.

Not heeding the speed limit, he headed back to his home. *Home*, he thought lamely, *a word used so loosely.* It was a monstrosity. A home passed down in his family that had fallen into disrepair. Five bedrooms, a formal dining room, a sunroom, and so many 'amenities,' and it was falling apart around him. He could not find the desire to repair it. He knew he had less than two years left before he could get out from under it. Seeing the tree-lined drive coming up on his left, he whipped into the lane and drove up the quarter-mile driveway to the circular drive. The broken fountain in the middle was dried out and crumbling.

Stopping in the circular drive in front of his house, he realized how badly he hated himself for what he had allowed to happen all those times in the brothel. He could not believe he had just sat there and wished he could say now that he had gotten her out. Wished he could say that he had saved her when he had the opportunity. Finding her behind the dumpster with her body bruised and broken made him so sick. He sat trying to think of every possible way he could have saved Hope before he found her that night, and every idea he came up with seemed to be filled with flaws that could have gotten one or both of them killed. Then he sardonically realized that one of them had gotten killed.

He slammed his car into park and jumped out of it, slamming the door. He cringed when he heard a clink and realized that his seatbelt had not had enough time to retract and he had tried to slam the door closed on it. Wondering how likely it was that he had chipped the paint, he whipped around just as he heard his phone ring. He jumped and reached for his gun, cursing when he realized that it was only his phone. Still caught up in potential escape routes. The sound of the phone ringing startled him from his reverie. Shaking his head, he answered the phone with a curt, "What?!"

"I do not have long, I have a favor to ask. I need a simple yes or no," the man on the other line stated.

Joe recognized the voice but could not place it. "Ask."

"Will you take the package and protect it with your life? Medical should be handled," he said brusquely.

Not abnormal to receive calls such as this, but confused by the medical, he hesitated before responding. Checking the caller ID, he saw that it said 'Private.' As he started to say no, he felt a breeze caress his hair and what smelled like daffodils fill his nose. "Yes," he heard himself respond, surprising himself and the man on the other end of the line.

"The package will arrive in five minutes. Please move it quickly to the most secure location possible."

As Joe started to ask where it would be delivered to, the call disconnected. Attempting to call the number back, he was not surprised when he got an automated message saying that the number was disconnected. He made his way to his front door when he realized that he still had not shut the car door properly. Muttering curses under his breath, he turned around and headed back to his car when he heard a car at the end of the drive. Rushing to his jeep, he ripped open the passenger door and pulled out his gun. Crouching down, he waited to see who would be arriving at his front door. A sedan he recognized pulled in, and he was not at all surprised when a man he recognized stepped out.

"Hello Henry," Joe called out, placing his gun in the waistband of his jeans at the small of his back. Walking cautiously over to Henry, he wondered how he knew where he lived. Not sure that he could trust him, he stopped ten paces from the car.

Henry looked from Joe to the house and back to Joe, he grimaced. "I am not sure this location will work, unless there is something that you are hiding inside of the house."

"Listen, I don't give a damn what you think of my house. What are you doing here? Let's get this handled quickly, I am expecting someone." Joe was irritated that Henry had shown up at his home and insulted it. Turning, he looked at the house and realized that he should not be irritated or insulted. The house looked like a piece of junk. Turning back around at the sound of the car door, he expected to see Henry getting back into his car to drive away, when he removed a person from the back seat. They had a hood over their head, concealing their identity. Joe immediately got nervous.

"What the hell is going on here?" he asked angrily.

"Would you calm down? You said you would accept the package. I am here with the package. Are you saying you will no longer accept it?" he emphasized 'package' with a grating tone. "I need to know now before this goes any further. If you say no, you will never see me ever again. You say yes, and you and I are going to be seeing each other once a week," Henry responded firmly yet urgently.

Momentarily stunned, Joe nodded his head in acquiescence and moved towards the front door.

"You know, most people close the door on their vehicle before going into their house," Henry tilted his head towards Joe's driver door. Embarrassed, Joe turned back around and headed back to his jeep. Retracting his seatbelt, he shut and locked the door. Striding towards his front door, he unlocked the three bolts, pushing open the door as barks rang out through the house.

Henry was pulled to a stop by the person in his arms as he tried to push them into the home. Their shaking and whimpering could be heard. Joe cocked his head sideways, looking at Henry before shouting, "Hush, it's just me." The barking immediately stopped. Henry refused to enter Joe's home, instead pushing the person into Joe's arms.

"I'll be in touch," he called over his shoulder as he walked back down towards his car.

Joe had no idea if this person was a hostile or someone who was just needing protection. Beyond irritated, he started to pull the person into his house, not certain where he should put them. He dragged them up the stairs to the bedroom next to his and shoved them inside. Shutting off the light, he started to walk out when the sound of his phone startled the person in front of him. Putting the phone to his ear, he growled, "Yes?"

"Almost forgot, package comes with presents. Left them on your front porch. Take care of her. I am trusting you with her." The sound of the phone once again disconnecting, was nearly enough to send Joe into a fit of rage. Turning around angrily, he ripped the hood off.

"Hope!" he gasped.

Henry was arguing with himself as he called Joe back to mention the presents. Should this be a man that he trusted or was this someone who was going to be leaving at the first sign of strife? He was so focused on dropping the bags off that he almost missed the sound of his personal cell ringing. Jumping down from the porch and rushing to his car, he reached through the driver side window to answer. Trying to sound like he was not breathless, he cleared his throat before answering.

"Hello, this is Henry…"

"Okay, so what are we doing? Are you back to stay? Or are you just going to disappear again? You kicked me out of the room with my niece; wouldn't let me hold her, wouldn't let me do anything to help with the funeral preparations. I got a simple text from you saying when the ceremony would be and that was it. I asked you multiple times who you were via text and even called you. You are throwing off so many mixed signals, I have absolutely no idea what to do."

"Hello, my pet," Henry said softly as he dragged the last of the bags from the car. He still had bags from the store where he had run into Jelissa and Joe. "I'll be by at 6 tonight to pick you up for dinner. Wear your scrubs, I will drop you off at work for the start of your shift. Before you even ask, yes, I will pick you up at the end of your shift as well." Hanging up the phone, he smiled to himself knowing that this was not the kind of conversation that Jelissa had expected. He half-wondered if she would be ready when he got there and was intrigued by both possibilities.

Chapter 12

"I never thought I would see you again," Joe gasped. He wanted so badly to reach out and hug Hope but was not sure it would be appropriate. Going to put his hands into his pockets, he could not help but reach out towards her. Shaking his head, he started to turn when he heard a sound come from Hope. Turning back around to look at her, he heard her whisper:

"Please do what you were going to do."

Stunned, Joe thought better about hugging her, afraid it would overwhelm her, and instead reached up his hand to cup her cheek. Pain filled Hope's eyes before she could close them. Pressing her cheek to his palm, she raised her own hand and placed it atop his, next to her cheek. A solitary tear slipped down her cheek. His thumb reached out to catch it and wipe it away, the movement causing Hope to catch her breath and take a step back. She glanced around the room looking for an escape.

As she looked around, Joe did too, and he was ashamed by what he saw. There was no furniture to be found in the room. The only bed in the house was his. Taking a chance, he reached out his hand to Hope, wishing with every part of him that she would trust him and take his hand. She took a bracing breath and placed her hand in his upturned palm; both of them were surprised by the shock felt with the touch. Smiling to each other, he turned to lead her out of the room.

Following Joe into the other room, Hope could not conceal her interest in the rooms around her. She had always dreamed of owning a home like this. She and her mom were not poor, but wealth was something she was definitely not accustomed to. As she walked, she started noticing the age of the home.

Maintenance had not been a priority for those who had lived here, and she wondered how Joe was able to have this home. Glancing at him, she saw him staring at her face. Blushing, she dropped her eyes.

"I am sorry, I was not trying to pry. I think your home is beautiful. Or is this even a home?" she queried. "The other man, I never saw who it was, told me he was taking me to a safe house."

"Well, I would like to think this will be a safe house for you. That other man was Henry. The man who was there the night..." stuttering to a stop, Joe looked at her again. "What happened?"

Shaking her head silently, Hope was thrown back to that night. The pain that was radiating from her shoulder was so excruciating and seeing her own blood saturating her shirt had caused her to lose consciousness. As far as she could tell, she had been taken away from her aunts for their own protection. Based on where her body had been found, she was too much of a liability. Therefore, unless she was protected, she would forever be a target. Explaining all this to Joe, he was astounded that Henry had accomplished such a feat without Jelissa or Nicole finding out.

"I want to hug you. To know that you are okay. I want to take care of you, but I don't want to smother you either," Joe burst out.

Hearing this, Hope looked away. She wanted to be able to accept a hug from someone again, but every time she thought about someone touching her, it made her feel ill. The thought of hugging Joe specifically made her feel so ashamed. He deserved someone who had not been touched by so many. She had no idea how many sexual partners she had had. She had been chosen for groups often, as long as they did not want a woman who would scream. She had not screamed until that last night. Even now, she could hear the sounds. Shuddering, she started to close off when she felt Joe squeeze her hand.

"I am not trying to pressure you. I just want you to know that you're safe," Joe reassured.

"Thank you, I am just not quite ready at this time. I hope you can understand and do not feel as though I am treating it as a personal affront to you," Hope intoned.

Smiling, Joe shook his head. "No, I will not take it as a personal affront. Thank you for wanting to reassure me that I am not a problem. But, please know, I am here for you in whatever capacity that you need, okay?"

"That is very kind of you and also completely unnecessary. Once my shoulder heals from the gunshot, I will be more than happy to take my leave and not be a burden anymore." At her words, Joe's entire countenance fell. Still embarrassed and ashamed that he had not kept her safe.

"I am so sorry that I did not keep you safe that night. I should have protected you. Just as your mom had asked me to. I promised her I would keep you safe, and I got you shot." Hanging his head, Joe closed his eyes, still seeing the woman fall to the ground after being shot by Henry. Pandemonium broke out in the hospital at that time. He ran trying to get to the room as fast as he could. He saw Henry shoving Jelissa and Nicole into the bathroom in the room, telling them to lock the door. Joe attempted to enter the room, when Henry saw him and shoved him out, yelling he had failed her. He tried to fight to get in when the officers who had been sitting in the waiting room came running down the hall, guns drawn.

Neither of the men were familiar to Joe and he had hated leaving, except he could not chance being seen by one of the officers. Rapidly retreating down the hall, he headed to the entrance. Hearing a code blue called over the speakers, he stepped into a broom closet down from Hope's room. Waiting five minutes, he stepped out when the sound of sobbing reached his ears. Sitting on the floor in the hallway outside Hope's room, Jelissa, Nicole, and Karen were crying with every ounce of their being. Being pulled back to the present by pressure on his wrist, he lifted his head to see Hope staring at him, worry evident on her face.

"Where did you just go?" she asked tentatively.

"I was just remembering that night. The night of your...oh!" grabbing her hand, he started to pull her towards his bedroom. He felt her pull back, the fear she was experiencing was palpable. "Please, trust me," he whispered hoarsely.

She looked from his face to his hand on hers, then back to his face. Nodding quickly, she wove her fingers in his and followed him. When they entered the bedroom, he started to let go of her hand when she grabbed tighter. Turning his head, he smiled at her before pulling her to his nightstand. The gift bag on the stand was slightly dusty. He handed the bag to her bashfully. "It isn't much, but I saw it and decided it would suit you. I was out grabbing it when you got hurt."

Suddenly extremely shy, Joe was extremely disappointed when he felt Hope pull away but did not want to push her too fast, too soon. "I need both hands to open the present. My left shoulder cannot hold much weight yet until I finish recuperating from the gunshot. No, before you say sorry, I do not blame you. I blame the woman who held the gun. Sarah or something, I believe."

Shaking his head slightly, "No, it was Susannah. A nurse on that floor. I am still trying to decide what made her decide to shoot you. I am so pleased she was not used to shooting, otherwise, you could have been hurt a lot worse."

Shivering, Hope was startled when she remembered the impact of the bullet. Then, she started laughing. A chill running down her back with the events of the last five months running through her mind. Who could have thought she would be in this situation? Four-and-a-half months ago, her biggest concern was the forcing of girls to wear skirts as part of a uniform. Now, knowing how much it covered and how relatively modest it was, she would kill to have just worn those uniforms and having had a normal senior year. Shaking herself from her thoughts, she sat on the chair beside the bed and peeked inside the gift bag.

"What is it?" she asked tentatively. Shrugging, Joe plopped on the edge of his bed, watching her with a small smile on his face. "Why are you smiling?" she asked, feeling the walls close in around her as she felt his eyes on her. Her hands clenched into fists around the bag. The edges digging into her palms. She could hear him answering but could not hear what he was saying, as the probing look he was giving her became too intense. She felt her hands start to hurt and she could not understand why she threw what was in her hands away from her. Seeing the bag crash to the floor and something yellow fall from it, she came tumbling back to Earth. Looking up at Joe, she saw the hurt on his face.

He bent down and picked up the bag. Walking calmly out of the room, he headed down the stairs. Not understanding, Hope got up to follow him. Stumbling down the stairs, she reached the bottom just as she heard the trash can close, then the back door slam shut. Following the noise, she walked into the kitchen and saw the most beautiful yellow silk she had ever seen, hanging out of the garbage can. Cautiously entering the kitchen, she peeked out the back door before opening the can and pulling the bag out. The scarf was profoundly beautiful and soft with intricate lace patterns on the end.

Reaching into the can to pull the gift bag out, she felt something hard in the bottom of the bag. Curious, she pulled out a movie; a comedy, she mused. It was one she had already seen. The last movie that her mother had taken her to see in the theatre. All about bridesmaids who had almost ruined a wedding by fighting and getting food poisoning. She smiled softly, then laying the scarf and movie down, she started to head out the back door, when she stopped and grabbed the scarf before cautiously opening the back door. The screen squeaked as it opened, causing Joe, who was standing on the porch, to turn.

He had been standing there, one leg bent behind the other, arms braced on the porch, eyes searching the land beyond the porch. She could see the determination, and something else. A loneliness, perhaps, in his stance. She almost regretted him turning to look at her as the door opened. She wavered, then decided she owed him an apology. Stepping quietly to the porch railing, she placed her hands on the rail as he had before. One holding gently to the scarf.

"It's beautiful. Thank you," she uttered softly.

"You don't have to. I saw your face. It was no big deal. Just something I grabbed quickly," Joe replied, not masking the lie or the pain on his face as he spoke.

"I said, it's beautiful. I am sorry that I threw it on the floor. I was not trying to reject your gift and the thought you put into purchasing it for me. You did not know me enough to have been able to select such a perfect gift for me," she said gratefully.

Startled when she said perfect gift, he turned to look at her. Then, he settled his hands on the railing as well to avoid having to look at her. The sunlight had caught her hair just right, it looked as though it were on fire. She was stunning. A completely inappropriate thought for him to have. He started to tell her it was nothing, then decided that if he was going to successfully care for her, he needed to be honest. Taking a deep breath, he started to thank her, when he felt her hand tentatively touch his. Tensing, he did not move for fear of startling her. He did not know if he should reciprocate the touch or let her decide what she was comfortable with.

When Hope felt Joe tense beside her, she realized she was silly to have thought he was open to any sort of touch from her. She was 'damaged goods,' or so the woman at the house had told her repeatedly. Retracting her hand, she was startled when she heard him whisper, "Wait." Replacing her hand on the railing next to him, she held her breath, waiting to see what would happen. The noise of his cell phone in his pocket startled both of them. Joe cursed as he pulled out his phone, turning sharply at the same time to check his surroundings. Seeing nothing, he turned back to Hope as he answered the phone.

Hope had staggered back at the sound, thinking herself ludicrous for having been frightened by the sound of the phone. However, she could feel the anxiety start to kick in. Looking up at Joe, she could see the concern on his face as he came towards her. Faced with the potential of rejection, she raced into the house, through the kitchen, and back up the stairs. Reaching the top, she did not know which way to turn. She hastened to the only place she had felt safe so far: Joe's room. Running to the other side of his bed, she crouched down next to it, wrapping her hands around her knees and dropping her head to her arms.

Joe raced up the stairs after her, concerned by the call he had just received, but more concerned by the way that Hope had reacted to the sound. The fear that had crashed over her face was so heartbreaking that he feared he would not be the help she needed. He would need to call Henry as quickly as possible to see what the plan was. He wanted to call one of her aunts, then realized they did not know that she was alive. Pushing open each door as he came to it and not seeing her, panic started to rise in his chest; afraid someone had gotten into the house while he had been distracted outside and now they had taken her. Reaching his bedroom last, he pushed open the door. He did not see her, and the sound of his own heaving breaths drowned out hers. It was the sob coming from her that caught his ear as he moved to go out of the room. He felt his heart wrench in his chest as he made his way around the bed.

"Hope," he whispered gently. "What can I do?"

Hope lifted her head and stared at Joe; fear, anxiety, embarrassment, then finally acceptance and relief washing over her features. "Hold me," she pleaded.

Astonished, Joe knelt beside Hope. Lifting her gently, he went to place her on the bed, when she tensed. Cursing himself for his lack of consideration, he walked to the sofa and sat down with her on his lap. Wrapping his arms tightly around her, he held her as she sobbed for the first time in two weeks. Her breathing gradually lessened and lengthened, until she fell asleep in his arms.

Chapter 13

While Hope slumbered in Joe's arms, safe for the first time in weeks, Jelissa felt more out of her element than she thought possible. She called Nicole multiple times, asking her to come over and help her decide if she should wear something cute or follow his directions and wear scrubs. Should she do her make-up like any other day or should she do something special? Too many questions were running through her mind. She considered calling Karen, but the jealousy she felt over Henry having pulled her into the hug made it extremely difficult. At 5:45 pm, she gave up and just got ready for work. Deciding that he had probably just said that to get a rise out of her and would probably not show, she got dressed and decided she would take herself out to dinner instead.

By dinner, she meant stopping at the local golden arches and getting a head start on her rounds at the hospital. Ever since Nicole had walked out, Jelissa had to pick up a lot of patients and shifts until the hospital could decide what to do. The hospital had found that the trauma done to Nicole probably meant that she had some sort of PTSD. However, until she was ready and willing to get help, there really was nothing that they could do. Slipping on her comfortable tennis shoes, she glanced into the mirror next to the front door. Seeing bags under her eyes, she was grateful she would not be seeing anyone but patients tonight.

Running her fingers through her hair, she decided to braid it in a long rope down her back in order to keep it out of her face. Jelissa glanced down at the watch on her wrist, causing her to miss a few strands of hair. Glancing back up, she started to undo the braid to start over, when there was a knock on the door. Huffing, she quickly plaited the rest of her hair into a braid and pulled open the front door.

She gasped when she saw who was at the front door, having completely forgotten that Henry might show up. Angry with herself for not being gone before he got there, she proceeded to try and close the door when he reached a hand out to stop her. "My pet, you look lovely. I am surprised and pleased you are so prompt."

Grimacing at the endearment, she felt the coil of warmth begin again in the pit of her stomach. Not entirely unwelcome, but definitely not unpleasant either. Deciding to just go and get a free meal out of it, she grabbed her keys and phone and dropped them into her pockets on her scrub top. The bumble bees on her top seemed to dance along the shirt with the movement. Mesmerized, Henry dropped his glance, realizing too late how it would look.

"Do they meet your approval then?" Jelissa sarcastically murmured. Straightening her spine, she marched out of the house, shutting the door behind her. Intentionally leaving her purse behind. Feeling a chill go down her back, she glanced over her shoulder to see Henry staring at her back as she walked down her drive. Enjoying the thrill, she threw her head back and laughed. Getting to his car, she moved to open her door when she felt his hand on her arm. Shaking his head wordlessly, he pulled open the door. Taking her hand, he helped her into the car and shut the door after her.

Taking a deep breath as he walked around the car, he wondered at the intelligence of taking her on a date. He needed help, and he was hoping she could be the one to help him. Sliding into the driver's seat, he went to turn the key in the ignition when he realized it was not there. Turning to look at Jelissa, she smiled, dangling the keys from her forefinger and thumb. He reached for them as she pulled back.

"Where are we going?" she questioned.

"You will see when we get there. Please give me the keys," Henry insisted. Frustration starting to rise inside of him. The frustration surprised him, as he usually could keep cool.

"You once told me that you were going to hurt me. That you did not want to, but you felt it was inevitable. So, I want to know where we are going so that I can text it to Nicole," she held the keys out of reach as she said this.

Sighing resignedly, he took the phone and texted Nicole the name of a local restaurant. It was a Wednesday, and he wanted the free piece of pie that was offered. Once he saw that it was sent, he deleted it from Jelissa's phone so that she would not be able to see. Smiling wickedly, he snatched the keys from her hand, turned on the ignition, and pulled away from the house. As he pulled away, he thought he saw someone approach the house, but when he looked again, he saw no one. Deciding that he was seeing things, he relaxed into the drive.

Reaching his hand across, he captured Jelissa's in his and brought it to the gear shift. Placing her palm on it, he laced his fingers with hers. He was surprised when she did not pull her hand from his. Rather, she seemed to relax into the seat further. Realizing that she was calmed by his touch brought a twinge to his heart when he realized what he was going to ask her to do. Pushing it to the back of his mind, he was planning to wait until the end of the night to ask. Sitting in silence, Henry prepared himself for the questions or chatter he was sure to come. In his experience, talking was a must, especially for a first date. When questions were not forthcoming, he stole a glance at Jelissa to see her head leaned back against the seat as she slept silently.

Smiling, Henry continued the drive, content with her ability to sleep around him. The initial tug to his heart pulling a bit harder, until he shoved it from his mind. Pulling into the parking lot, he wondered if he should wake her or just let her sleep. Realizing that she would be having an extremely long night, he decided he would wake her so that she would have the energy needed to make it through the night. Picking up their joined hands, Henry brought them to his lips, turning them so he could kiss the center of her palm. When she did not react, he started to nibble on her fingertips before drawing her forefinger gently into his mouth and biting down.

Waking quickly to see her finger in Henry's mouth, she stared in wonder as she felt his tongue soothe away the bite. Pulling her finger from his mouth, he placed a kiss on her finger and then her palm again, before placing her hand back on her lap. Getting out of the car, he walked around the side while she sat in stunned silence.

Certain that she had imagined what had just happened, Jelissa was startled when Henry opened her car door. Placing her hand in his outstretched palm, she was pulled from the car. Shutting the door, he pushed her back against it. Eyes growing wide, Jelissa watched as Henry leaned towards her mouth. At the last minute, he instead went cheek to cheek before whispering in her ear, "You intrigue me and excite me more than you know." Catching her earlobe in his mouth, he nipped it with his teeth, giving it a tug before pulling back. Jelissa's quick intake of breath showed him that he was not the only one feeling things. The question that was pressing at him was whether this was just lust and circumstance or something more.

Calmly placing her right hand in the crook of his left arm, Henry escorted Jelissa into the restaurant. Recognizing him, they immediately seated Henry in a back-corner booth. He ordered them both a water with lemon before the hostess left. Jelissa, upon hearing this, was broken from her revere. "I have no idea what is happening here. I am not certain if I like it yet. But I can tell you that you intrigue and excite me too. I want to see where this goes, but I am terrified that you really are going to hurt me, and being hurt by a man is not something that I think I can come back from again."

Pleased with her honesty, he reached across the table and grabbed her hand. Reassured, Jelissa continued, "You make me feel things that I have not felt in years. Things I have not felt since Eric…" Her voice broke on the name. "He hurt me quite terribly. I loved him with every bit of me and he cheated on me. I gave him another chance and he did it again. I decided one more chance. One more opportunity, then I found out I was pregnant; and I was hurt and scared but so hopeful that he would take care of me. That he would love me the way that I deserved. One night, I was having a particularly difficult night. The morning sickness I had been experiencing was particularly bad. I was needing him and his support. I called him, but he did not answer. That is when the first wave of pain hit me."

The waitress stopped by with the waters ready to ask if they were wanting to order when Henry simply shook his head, never taking his eyes off Jelissa. Hurting for her and imagining all the ways that he would hurt Eric forever hurting Jelissa.

Jelissa took a quick sip of her lemon water, never letting go of Henry's hand. Her focus was in the past, but she clung to Henry's hand to keep herself in the present. He was quickly becoming her anchor and it scared her. "I waited for half an hour, by then dinner had gotten cold, but I had not started eating because I could not seem to keep anything down. I started getting cramps in my stomach and rushed to the bathroom, unsure whether I would be sick. That's when I noticed the blood." Gulping, Jelissa took a breath, needing to finish the story. She did not know what had compelled her but knew that now that she had started, she would need to finish. "I called him again. I needed him to take me to the hospital, something was wrong with the baby. He did not answer again. I kept calling and calling him, needing him to answer, as I slowly grabbed a towel and walked out to my car.

I was hoping that he would show up at home as I was getting in the car and be there, only he never got there. I drove myself to the hospital and learned I had lost our baby. It was a girl. She would have been so beautiful. I was in the hospital room, having just been given the medicine to induce labor to fully miscarry the baby, when I got the call. I answered, so happy and relieved that he had called and could meet me at the hospital, when the man on the other side introduced himself as police and asked me if I was Eric's girlfriend, I confirmed it, and he told me that he had been in an accident. He had not made it. He was on his way home from his lover's apartment, pissed that I had called him so many times. He was coming home to break up with me when he hit black ice and spun off the road. He died on impact."

The waitress came to the table again, Henry glanced at Jelissa before quickly putting in an order for both of them. Squeezing her hand, he encouraged her to finish what she had started.

"She came to his funeral. After I did everything to prepare for it, I had to see her show up to the funeral. What's worse is she showed up with a swollen belly. She was pregnant with their child. Eric Junior. He is four-and-a-half now. I receive a card every year with his picture reminding me that I took his father away from him with my selfishness to have him with me that night. No one else knows that. No one else knows I lost my baby either. Kathryn Rose was going to be her name." Shaking her head slightly, she blushed with the realization of everything that she had shared. Henry stood up from the booth, releasing her hand. Hurt by the rejection, Jelissa dropped her head, emotionally exhausted, when she felt Henry pull her by her left hand to her feet. Wrapping her in a hug, Jelissa was encompassed in the warmest, safest hug she had ever experienced.

"What the hell are you doing to me, Jelissa?" He whispered hoarsely. "I don't know what to do with the feelings that are rolling through me and I am ashamed to admit this, but I am scared by what I feel because it is too soon." Tucking her forehead into Henry's neck, Jelissa kissed his chin before cuddling in tight. When someone cleared their throat next to them, Jelissa started to pull away, when Henry stopped her. Leaning forward, he rubbed his nose gently against Jelissa's before sitting down in the booth, next to her this time. He could not seem to stop touching her. Soups and salads were placed in front of them. Jelissa immediately started in, on the soup, savoring the potatoes with bacon bits. Quickly finishing her soup, she realized how exhausted she was and leaned against Henry's shoulder while she savored the flavor of the soup.

Slowly picking at the salad in front of her, she noticed that there appeared to be a vinaigrette of some sort on it. Pushing her fork into the green leaves, she tentatively brought it to her mouth, surprised when the flavor of blueberries exploded across her tongue. Lifting her head, she quickly ate the salad as well. Surprising herself, as she usually would never order herself a salad. She looked over at Henry and saw that he had barely begun eating his. Life in the medical field had made her rush through a meal, never knowing when a medical emergency would occur. Henry chuckled, and continued to eat when he suddenly saw a fork stab into his salad and disappear into Jelissa's mouth. Watching her, he realized just how comfortable she was with him and he felt his heart go the edge, ready to take the leap.

He had secrets, though one in particular he needed to get taken care of before this goes any further with Jelissa. He wanted everything to be open and honest with her. He knew that if his pet found out before he had the opportunity to tell her, it could ruin everything. He did not know if he could live with himself if a secret or lie of his caused them to no longer be together. He was full of hope when it came to Jelissa. Scared out of his wits, but so excited by the prospect.

Pulling himself back, he glanced up and saw the waitress approaching their table. Anticipating the flavor exploding on his tongue, Henry ordered a cherry and apple pie, with a scoop of vanilla ice cream for each one. Glancing down to take another bite of his salad, he saw that over half of it was gone and Jelissa was sitting with innocence on her face. Laughing outright, he pushed the salad in front of her and saw her glancing at him in awe. "I have never heard you laugh," she said.

"I have a feeling you will hear me laugh often," he said confidently. 15 minutes later, they had finished their meals and were polishing off their pie, when Jelissa remembered that she had not brought her purse and suddenly felt guilty. When Henry simply stood up to walk out, she was concerned until he said to the hostess to put the bill on his tab and gave the waitress a $20 tip. Continuing out to the car, Henry once again opened the door for Jelissa before assisting her into the car. Reticent to release her hand, he gave it a quick squeeze before quickly shutting the door and jogging around the outside. Sliding into his seat, he glanced at Jelissa, where she waited with her hand once again in the air. Only this time it was empty, and she was simply waiting to hold his hand again. Grabbing it and kissing the inside of her wrist, he placed her hand, palm down on the gear shift again as they headed to the hospital.

When he parked, instead of simply dropping her off, she wondered what his intentions were. When he unbuckled, she did the same, and was startled and pleasantly surprised when he leaned quickly across the car and crushed his lips with hers. Pressing her into the seat, his hands dove into her hair. Slightly gripping it, he dipped his tongue into her mouth before withdrawing and nipping her lips until she whimpered. Pulling away slightly, he noticed that her eyes were half-closed and her lips were swollen. Kissing her eyes, the tip of her nose, and then her lips, one last time, he sat back in his seat. Squeezing her hand, he quickly got out of the car, going around the front so that he could see her the entire time. She sat waiting expectantly for him to open the door. When he opened it and helped her out, she surprised him by placing her arms around his waist and dropping her forehead to his chest.

"That was unexpected and so amazing. Thank you," she whispered.

Leaning down and kissing the crown of her head, Henry simply held her tightly for a moment before releasing her long enough to slide his hand down her arm to her hand. Walking her into the hospital, he promised her that he would be back in the morning to pick her up. Placing one last chaste kiss on her lips and then her forehead, he turned just in time to see a bald man round the corner of the hospital. He recognized him. Taking off after him, Henry pushed to the back of his mind the last few hours with Jelissa, focusing on the task at hand.

Chapter 14

The pain had dimmed to a dull throb. Trying to open her eyes, she felt the swollenness of her eyes and realized that she would not be opening her eyes for at least a couple of days. Trying to swallow, she realized how dry her mouth was. Wishing she could have water, she attempted to speak, when she felt the pain in her jaw. Realizing that it was most likely broken, she gave up trying to open her mouth.

She heard a cell phone beep and then voices laughing about someone getting ready for a date. Confused, she attempted to rise up when she felt ants crawling all over her legs, biting her. Crying out in pain, she realized that her legs had fallen asleep and were now waking. At her cry, the voices quieted down. She heard footsteps come to the door. Suddenly, light flooded into the room. The footsteps got closer. Hoping they would give her something to drink, she once again attempted to sit up, when she felt a foot connect with her ribs. Gasping, she fell once more to the floor. The pain grew so intense that she slipped back into the void.

Joe's arms were beginning to hurt, when he felt Hope stir in his arms. Unsure what to do, he had waited. When she suddenly tensed, he realized that fear would most likely cause her to react negatively. He was determined to respond politely and with understanding. It was when her body started to shake that he decided to speak. "Hope, it is just me, Joe."

At his voice, Hope immediately started to push away from him. Mortified that she had fallen asleep on him, she sat up and moved to the other end of the couch. Turning to look back at Joe, she watched as he leaned towards her and touched her cheek. Staring into his eyes, she allowed the touch to calm her. Closing her eyes, she started to take deep breaths, when she felt his lips press softly against hers. Startled, Hope's eyes flew open as she jumped off the couch. Turning to look at him and seeing his kind face, she was thoroughly disgusted that he had touched the lips that had done things she was so ashamed of. Running to his bathroom, she slammed the door and locked it before vomiting violently.

She heard the door to his bedroom close and his feet as he descended the stairs. Turning, she saw the bath and turned it on as hot as it would go. Ripping her clothes from her body, she climbed in. She relished the heat, hoping it would wash away the disgust she felt for herself. Seeing soap on the side of the tub, she started scrubbing as hard as she could, wanting to get rid of the feel of the hands that had touched her body. Fog started to fill the bathroom as she scrubbed. Turning off the water before it could reach the brim, she started to scrub, feeling more like she could not get clean.

Frustrated, she submerged herself under the scalding-hot water. The pressure on her ears gave her the feeling of isolation. She needed to feel clean. Focusing on her lungs, she felt them start to feel compressed. There was a pressure in her chest that started to increase. Steadily, she began releasing a little more air, dragging the moment out as long as she could. Suddenly, she was ripped from the bathtub. Spluttering, she found herself in Joe's arms. Pushing her from him, he grabbed a towel off the hook on the bathroom door and wrapped it around her, careful not to touch her skin. Reaching in to drain the tub, he withdrew his hand when he felt the heat. Throwing a scathing look at Hope, he reached back in, pulling the plug.

"Don't you ever pull a fucking stunt like that ever again!" he yelled. Stalking out of the bathroom, he slammed the door to the bedroom and pounded down the stairs.

Hope stood confused as she replayed everything in her head that had happened. Realizing how it probably looked to Joe, she started to head towards the door when she realized that he had shoved her from him. He had wrapped her in a towel so that he did not have to see her. Almost to the bedroom door, she stopped. Turning around, she hoped to find a robe or something to wear so that she could wash the clothes she had worn for the last two weeks. That is when she saw countless bags on the bed. Walking over cautiously and peering in, she started pulling clothes from the bags, all in her size. Everything she could possibly need. Baffled, she wanted to ask Joey about it, then thought now was not the time.

Finding a lot of cute outfits, she considered putting some on when she realized that her skin was quite sensitive. Glancing down, she noticed the redness to her skin and realized that through her reaction she had burned her skin. Wishing she had something to wear that would not hurt her skin, she turned to the wardrobe standing against the wall. Walking over to it, she hesitated before pulling open the doors. Seeing drawers inside, she started pulling them open until she found a pair of sweatpants with a drawstring. Pulling them out, she furtively glanced behind her before pulling them on. The soft material on the inside only slightly irritated her legs. Moving to close the drawer, she saw a t-shirt that looked very worn. Deciding that it would be comfortable, she quickly dropped the towel as she tossed the shirt over her head. Dropping her nose to the collar, she could smell him on the fabric. Deciding that she had already fully invaded his space, she went back to the top drawer where she had seen his socks and pulled out a pair. Pulling those on as well, she closed the wardrobe.

Picking the towel up from where she had dropped it on the floor, she walked back to the bathroom to hang it back up. Turning to look at herself in the mirror, she saw that her face was red from the heat of the water and her eyes were swollen from the tears she had not even realized she had cried. Going back out to the bags, she found a brush. Climbing up onto the bed, she crossed her legs and started brushing her hair. She hated the color and could not wait for it to grow out back to its natural blonde. Hearing the door open behind her, she tensed, before slowly drawing the brush back through her hair. She grimaced as she tried to work the knots from her hair. Having not brushed it for two weeks had done quite the damage.

She felt the bed dip behind her. Joe took the brush from her hand and started brushing her hair. Placing the brush at the top of her head, he started to drag the brush down. Quickly getting tangled, he was immediately contrite when he felt her wince in pain. She reached up and slowly extracted the brush from his hand before starting at the bottom and slowly working up. Seeing this, Joe once again reached forward and started to brush her hair. Neither said a word as he worked. Unsure whether they could talk to the other without saying anything hurtful. 15 minutes later, when he had finished brushing, she started to lean back against him when he stood up quickly. Realizing what she had started to do, she straightened and started rifling through the bags looking for a hair band. Seeing one, she tossed her hair up in a messy bun.

She turned to see where he had gone, catching him watching her as she put her hair up. Flustered, he suddenly stopped when he realized what she was wearing. "I'm sorry. My skin, it was sore. I needed something comfortable," she murmured, embarrassed. I can change if you'd prefer."

"No, it's fine. I am glad it is comfortable for you. We can go shopping tomorrow for anything else you might need," he replied. Going over to the couch on the side of the room, he started to push and pull it towards the door of the room.

"What are you doing?" she asked.

"Moving the couch to the other room. You can sleep in here. I will take the couch to one of the other rooms," he answered before once more starting to move the couch.

"Wait," she whispered. Then louder, "You can sleep on your bed, I can take the couch. Or I can just sleep on the floor, it's…"

"Absolutely not up for discussion. You are hurting. This is something I can finally do for you that I know would help you rather than hurt you."

"Then leave the couch in here. Please," she added quickly. Blushing, she dropped her gaze. "I do not want to bother your sleep, but I am hoping I will sleep better knowing that you are here. I…" she stumbled, "…I am scared to be alone."

Looking at her and realizing what a confession this was, he decided to respond with something that would have as little cause for further embarrassment as possible. "Oh, thank God, this couch was extremely heavy and I was not sure I was going to be able to get it all the way out of the room without embarrassing myself. That is also the only working bathroom at this time. I am sorry the accommodations are not very good, but your, uh, visit, was unexpected." Pushing the couch back to the wall, he straightened to catch her watching him this time. Deciding not to comment, he strode from the room in search of an extra pillow and blanket, hoping he had one. Otherwise, it would end up a very uncomfortable night. Walking back into the room, he saw her standing at the wardrobe slowly moving clothes over and hanging some of hers.

Silently, he walked up next to her and started consolidating what he had into three of the six drawers. She murmured a thank you as he worked. Walking away from the wardrobe, he snatched a pillow from the bed and the throw at the bottom to take to the couch, having been unsuccessful in finding any other bedding in the house. Turning, he saw that she had witnessed his actions. Grinning sheepishly, he tossed the pillow and throw on the couch. He asked her if she needed anything, she shook her head no and continued to organize her clothes into the wardrobe.

After his discussion with the bald man, Henry decided that it was time to call his superiors looking for directions for the ring he was trying to take down. If anything, he had realized tonight that he was not comfortable with using Jelissa to try and find the ring, but he was running out of options. Another girl had been taken. When Henry reached his supervisor, he quickly gave a run-down of what he had done with Hope, his lack of an update on Jelissa, and the information he had just forced from the bald man. They were highly displeased that he had not asked Jelissa and demanded he find a plant in 24 hours. Deciding that Nicole might work, he got into his car and headed to her home.

Pulling up at the end of her driveway, he saw that her car was not there and the lights were not on. Curious and concerned, he walked quickly up the drive. Knocking on the door, he then tried calling her. When she did not answer, he decided to try the door. When the handle turned, he turned to call for backup before entering the home and felt rather than saw the heat that blasted towards him as the home billowed smoke and flames from the front door, throwing him back from the porch. His last thought before he lost consciousness was that he would be letting down his pet by not picking her up from work in the morning.

Jelissa walked into work without knowing what to make of everything that had happened that night. It was exciting and scary, all at the same time. Deciding that she should focus on what was important, she shot a quick text to Nicole asking her to call her as quickly as possible. Deciding that she was no longer angry at Karen, she sent her a text as well, hoping that she would forgive the silence she had been given. When neither woman answered, Jelissa decided to start her rounds. It was two hours later, when she was just sitting down for the first time that a page came through asking for any available personnel to come to the ER. Rushing there, she waited with two others for the ambulance to arrive. She felt the adrenaline kick in as she waited, pleased she had eaten such a good meal before getting to work. Thinking of dinner brought a smile on her face. The ambulance arrived outside and she rushed out to meet the paramedic to receive the patient. When the back door opened and the man was brought out, she was startled to see Henry attached to the gurney. "No," she gasped before freezing.

The paramedic snapped at her to either help or move and it was enough to pull her from her fear. She refused to lose another person. Her phone chimed as she started to wheel him in, trying to determine the extent of his injuries. The burns prevalent on his body were bad enough. It was the gash across his forehead and the splinters of glass and wood that riddled his body that started to worry her more. He was unconscious and, according to the paramedic, had not woken but once on the drive over. She asked if he had said anything. They said they figured he was delirious, because he had simply said 'Sorry, pet.'

Hearing this, Jelissa became determined to not lose him. Pushing him to the same room Hope had been shot in, she started issuing orders to the nurses around her, getting everyone organized so that he could receive the best care possible. Any nurse she did not trust, she sent out of the room, not chancing a nurse being able to hurt him as they had Hope. Hearing her phone chime again, Jelissa grabbed it out, hoping it was Nicole. When she saw Nicole's name on the screen, she was thrilled and hoped she could get her to come in and help with Henry. Opening the text, she saw a picture. Nicole lying face down, tied up, with a note attached saying 'Call off your boyfriend, or she dies.'

Chapter 15

Three days had passed and Joe and Hope fell into a relatively calm and smooth routine. Every morning, Joe would get up early and shower and get dressed in the bathroom. Meandering downstairs, he would start the coffee and place the tea kettle on the stove for Hope. She would continue to sleep until he would come up to the room with her tea and a slice of toast. Gently calling her awake, they had found that the best way to wake her was for him to stand on the other side of the room and whisper her name, telling her it was him. He would then leave the room so that he would not see her if she reacted. This morning was no different.

Walking back down the stairs, Joe was debating how he would tell Hope that he would need to go into work today. Ever since the day at the press conference, he had not been allowed to go back to the brothel; the attention he had brought to himself angering the chief. Being presented with the opportunity to go back to the brothel again, was an opportunity he could not pass up. However, he could not decide if he should tell her that part or not. When he heard the creaking on the stairs, he glanced up, not expecting her to be coming down so soon. She walked into the kitchen barefoot with his sweatpants and shirt on, now hers, he supposed. Sitting down at the bar stool, she placed her toast on the counter and grasped the mug of tea between her hands, not looking at him.

"You have to go into work today, don't you?" she whispered.

Surprised, Joe looked up to see her grabbing her mug, her knuckles white. "Yes, I do." At his answer, he watched as Hope's body tensed even further. "What's wrong? Why does that make you so upset?"

"Please do not make me wear the hood," she cried desperately as she looked up and met his eyes. "I promise I will not run away, I will not leave, I will not do anything. I know I am here for my own safety. But I just cannot be locked in a room again and have that hood on my head!" Tears shimmered in her eyes that she refused to let fall.

"Hope," he started. "I threw away that hood. Disgusted that you had worn it here. I will not put you back in the hood, but you do need to understand the gravity of the situation that you are in. You absolutely cannot leave this house. There are people out there who are wanting to hurt you because you know the faces of the people who took you, who hurt you, and who…" he hesitated here.

"Who raped me?" her voice paused on this. Eyes calm, she said, "Who sat there and watched me get hurt and did nothing? Who would bring their e-reader and ignore me for an hour, making me feel like I was a disgusting thing." Looking at him squarely as she said this, she saw him grimace. Without remorse, she continued, "Yes, I know. I am not stupid. I know the severity of the situation I am in. Aunt Jelissa purchased me notebooks while at the store. I have been writing down descriptions of the people who took me. I have written down tattoos, scars, sounds of voices, and anything that I could to help you find who you need," Hope replied. There was a calmness and a determination in what she was saying. She was not going to back down. Joe felt a sense of pride come over him, realizing that she would be willing to do this.

"May I see it?" he asked gently.

"No," Hope was vehement in her response. She refused to give away this information until she figured out just how much she could trust Joe. She remembered what her mom said in her letter, but she refused to allow herself to be used again.

Nodding his head, Joe got up and refilled his coffee mug. Pointing to a memo pad on the counter, "There is a pen and pad of paper there. Let me know if you need anything while I am gone. I will stop and pick it up. If you promise that you will stay put, I would be happy to let you have free reign of the house. Just be careful, this house is not put together well. Also, I know I have introduced you to Athena a few times over the last couple days, but she is to stay in her room. I am still not sure she will not try to protect the house from you and I do not want you hurt." Shaking his head in disgust, he turned to walk away, when he caught sight of the look on her face.

"I can explore the house?" she asked in wonder.

Baffled, Joe was not sure how to respond. "Yes, while you are here, this is your home. Do and go where you'd like. Just please keep the doors locked and do not explore the land while alone. There are over 100 acres out there and it would be easy to get lost." Shaking his head slightly, he thought of all the ways she could get hurt. Considering calling in and instead having them come here, he turned and started to withdraw his permission and just stay, when he saw happiness on her face. He was momentarily stunned. Sliding the notebook over to Hope, he tossed her the pen too. "I am going to go get dressed now."

Not even looking up, Hope started scribbling away on the notepad. Curious, Joe walked over to look at the pad, when she chuckled and covered it with her hand. "No peeking."

Joe smiled and walked from the room. Feeling his phone vibrate, he had turned off the obnoxious ringing, he pulled it out to see a private caller. Hoping it was Henry, he answered quickly. "This is Joe…"

"Praise God, I was hoping it was you. This is Jelissa. I need your help. It's Nicole. She's been taken." Stopping in his tracks, Joe glanced down the stairs to Hope. Not wanting her to overhear the conversation, he rushed to his room.

"What happened? Are you okay?" Joe asked quickly. Throwing some clothes on, he hoped he could get this sorted before Hope came up the stairs. Jelissa did not know about Hope yet, and Hope did not need to hear about what was happening with Nicole. Thinking quickly, he asked Jelissa to tell him everything she knew. That is when she mentioned about Henry being injured and unconscious in the hospital. It was a good thing he had woken in the ambulance. However, the fact that he had not woken since then severely concerned her.

Turning quickly to head back out the door, he saw Hope standing there. "I'll be there as soon as I can, Jelissa," Joe said before hanging up the phone. Catching Hope's eyes, he walked towards the door. Expecting her to stop him, he was surprised when she simply stepped to the side, lips pressed into a thin line. Walking into the room, she went straight to the bathroom and locked the door. Thirty seconds later, he heard the shower turn on. Heaving a sigh, Joe headed down the stairs.

Getting to the kitchen, he started to walk out the door, when he remembered her list. Grabbing it from the counter, he shoved it in his pocket before going out the back door. Locking it and double-checking to make sure it was firmly closed, he walked around the entire perimeter of the house checking doors and windows. Seeing that all was secure, he walked briskly to his jeep before leaving. As a last-minute thought, he honked twice before taking off down the drive. Deciding he would see Jelissa first, he headed to the hospital. This time, he kept his speed below the requirement to not draw attention to himself.

Parking at the hospital, he realized what an issue this could cause, when he saw someone approaching his vehicle. As she approached, she continuously glanced over her shoulder. When an officer came outside and nodded at her, she held her head up higher and walked on, this time with more confidence and determination. Climbing into his passenger seat, the first thing she did was punch him in the arm.

"I cannot believe you would just abandon all of us like you did. Seeing you at the cemetery, and you don't even bother to come over and say hi! What is wrong with you?" Jelissa berated.

"I felt, feel, responsible," he said. Annoyed with himself for slipping up, he quickly tried to address the issue at hand: Henry and Nicole. "What is it that you are wanting me to do? I understand what you want done with Nicole. Find her and save her. With Henry, I do not understand."

"Henry said you guys work for the same company. I need you to get ahold of your boss and make sure they know what happened so they can investigate the fire at the house. Arson showed up, but I cannot get any information from them because I am not related to her. I figure that you are some sort of law enforcement officer and can get more information than I can," Jelissa reasoned.

Uncertain how much he would be able to do, he reassured Jelissa before asking the question that was pressing on his mind. "The officer standing at the door, I recognize him. He was there the night Hope was brought in, and he was also at the store when the three of us shopped for Hope. I saw him nod to you. Who is he?"

"His name is Nate. He has apparently been working with Henry on the sex trafficking ring and was there the night the bomb went off at Nicole's house. He wanted to lend his hand with anything that he could so that I would not be overly stressed. To be honest, I am not certain that I can trust him, so I have been reticent to lean on him at all." Looking over at him, she remembered that she still slipped up and called him Baldy. Something definitely seemed off about him, however, she could not place it.

"Okay, I will do some digging. I want to know why he was following us when we were at the store and whom he was following." Now, the dilemma sprung up about what he would and could say about Henry. He could tell that they cared for each other, but Henry was lying, so it did not sit well with Joe. As he started to say something, he watched Jelissa tense. "What's wrong?"

Jelissa quickly ducked down in the seat. "He just signaled to me that we are being watched. I need you to drive out of here and leave. Do not come back. Next time, we will need to meet in private. Just, please, find Nicole for me and do what you can about Henry. I don't know what I would do if I lost him," she shuddered. Opening the door, she prepared to exit, when she was stopped by Joe.

"You love him," Joe whispered in awe.

Startled, Jelissa turned to tell him no when she realized she could not. Trembling at this thought and the fact that she had just met him, she quickly exited the car. Hunching down, she snuck between cars and made a hasty getaway. Standing at the last moment, when she felt she could get away without making it obvious where she had come from.

Joe watched her leave, unsure what to do about the entire situation. Heading into work, he decided to do some detective work when he realized that he had not gotten the picture of Nicole or the information about Henry. Everything seemed so backwards and he wondered where his mind was, when he realized that all he could think about was bringing home yellow daffodils and whether Hope would be happy when he got home.

Disgusted with himself, he drove quickly to a local sushi restaurant and headed inside.

Trying to get back into a routine had proved almost fruitless. Every day, there was a reminder of the people that Karen had lost. She was an executor of an estate and had done nothing with it. It had been almost three weeks since the funeral and she had not been able to make it to the house yet. Terrified that she would be overwhelmed with the memories she had made there with Faith, Karen tried hard to push the memories away and focus on her four children and on work. However, every time she saw a young woman Hope's age, she could not help but remember everything that Hope had gone through.

She could feel herself going through the routine every day. Get up, make lunches for the kids, make lunch for her husband Mike, and then get herself her lunch. Go wake up the kids the first time. Go back and empty the dishwasher and back to wake up the kids a second time and wake up Mike. Then back to load up the dishwasher and start the coffee. Once all the backpacks were on the counter with the lunch boxes inside, she would go to the bedrooms one by one and get the kids up officially. One at a time, she would dress them and take them to get their teeth brushed; the twins were always the most fun. They would tease her about which child was whom. Her eldest, a 12-year-old boy, always headed to the shower quickly to beat his father to it.

Karen had cereal ready this morning to get their energy in; she had bowls of yogurt with sliced strawberries and bananas mixed in. Setting up the bowls at the counter, she checked the clock. Seeing that the time was later than she had thought, she rushed to the back rooms to see what was taking them so long. Getting to the first room and not seeing her kids, she panicked, running from room to room before ending up going to the last bedroom: hers and Mike's. Walking in, she was startled when she heard "Surprise!" shouted. Not understanding the occasion, as it was not her birthday and it was not her anniversary.

116

Looking quickly to Mike, she smiled happily and hugged her kids.

"We wanted to thank you for everything that you do for us every morning. You are what makes this family so amazing and strong. We do not take enough time to thank you for everything that you do," her eldest said. Tears sprang to Karen's eyes at the words, amazed that they had noticed that she needed this so much. She had fallen into a routine where she had stopped recognizing who she was.

"Thank you, I am so grateful and so overjoyed that you all have done this for me. I love all of you so much! I am sorry that I have been in a bit of a funk since Faith went away. It has not been easy, but you guys have been there for me and I cannot even express how much you all mean to me," Karen replied.

Each of her kids gathered around her with cards saying 'thank you' and different candy. It was not lost on Karen that each child had a different bag of candy, the kind they liked. One of the twins spoke up asking if she would share. Smiling with tears in her eyes, she nodded before meeting Mike's eyes over the top of the children's heads. He leaned in and gave her a sweet kiss, placing his palm on her cheek. Leaning into it, she felt calm come over her. Deciding it was time to get Nicole and Jelissa together, she thought out what they could do to make the biggest difference. Deciding that they could not do it alone, she wondered if either of the women had a way to contact Joe or Henry.

Hope stood in the shower, allowing the water to run over her. Knowing that Joe would not be there, she decided to take her time. Before, she always rushed because she did not want to chance him coming inside and seeing her. This sharing a bathroom was getting to be too much of a nuisance. Then, remembering her plan, she quickly shut off the shower grabbing the robe on the door and putting it on. Tossing her hair up in a bun without bothering to dry or brush it, she walked in the robe to the bed. When she got there, she realized that she could hear what sounded like someone moving around downstairs. Nausea immediately hit her and she realized that she had no means of protecting herself.

Considering hiding under the bed, she realized that this would get her nowhere. She was done hiding, she was done running, and she was done being scared. Going to the bedroom door, she quickly made her way down the stairs, stepping on what felt like every creak in the floor. Fleetingly, she decided that this would be one of the first things she would fix if she survived whoever was downstairs.

Reaching the bottom step, she hesitated when she saw a shadow in the doorway; the person appeared to be crouching down. Taking a deep breath, she started to take a step down when they suddenly leapt in front of her. Her scream rang out through the house.

As quickly as her scream began, it stopped and turned into laughter. She was then pounced on and licked furiously by the most beautiful German Shepherd she had ever seen. Raising her hands to cover her face, she tried to fend off the attack and barely succeeded, because she was so out of breath from the laughter. She had yet to meet Athena without Joe being present. Whenever they went to the room he was keeping Athena in, Hope would stand by the door and watch them interact. Joe had been worried that Athena might attack and had not wanted her to hurt Hope. He had kept her locked up in a room downstairs. Turning to look, she saw that the door was open. Concerned, she walked over and peeked in. Seeing nothing, she walked further into the room. Athena stood by the door, refusing to go in.

Looking back at her, she watched as Athena proceeded to lie down, then start rolling around on her back. Deciding that there was no threat, Hope headed back towards her, then saw that the door handle was covered in slime. Looking from the handle to Athena, Hope realized that she had used her mouth to open the door. "Smart girl, Athena," Hope cooed. Athena's tail started thumping on the floor while staring at Hope.

Walking out to the solitary couch in the house, she sat down with Athena next to her. Hopping up, she ran to the kitchen to get the memo pad off the counter to start making a list of things she wanted to work on. Settling back down on the couch, Hope crossed her legs and placed the pad on her right knee before patting the cushion next to her. Athena glanced behind her, then jumped up on the couch next to Hope, laying her head down on Hope's left knee.

Feeling content, Hope started to work on the list. There was so much to do, but she did not know how long she would be here. Scribbling furiously, she started adding sketches and decorations as she went room by room. When Athena rose her head up quickly, Hope decided to see if she needed to be let out. Walking to the back door, she lifted her hand to open the door, when she heard footsteps on the porch. Athena started to growl.

Hope looked from Athena to the door and slowly backed away. When the door handle started to shake, she turned and raced down the hallway. Athena close at her heels. When she started to head up the stairs, Athena corralled her and shoved her towards the front, before quickly diverting her to the kitchen door. That's when she heard the crash and splintering of wood as the front door was slammed open. Having no time to even put on shoes, Hope ran out the back door. Seeing the tree-line a few hundred yards away, Hope dashed towards it, following Athena. She had almost reached the tree line when she heard the shouts. Not even turning, she crashed into the trees.

She kept her eyes in front of her, following Athena, trusting her inexplicably. When Athena suddenly halted and hunkered down, Hope did the same. Suddenly realizing that she could not breathe, she started to try and calm her breathing. Athena started nuzzling her hand with her nose, licking her hand. Turning, Hope grabbed Athena in a hug and buried her face in her neck. Feeling Athena tense beside her, Hope quickly released her, looking for her cue. Athena shoved her with her body and took off into the woods again.

She ran as fast as her legs could carry her. Her lungs were burning and the pain in her shoulder was overwhelming, but she kept running. She could hear shouts behind her, which pushed her to run faster and farther than she realized she was even capable of doing. She noticed she could hear someone behind her, close on her heels. Suddenly, her body was slammed to the ground by someone tackling her from behind.

Before she even had time to scream for Athena, a hand was clamped over her mouth.

Jelissa rushed back into the hospital, making her first stop back at Henry's room. She did not know what was happening with her and the realization that she loved him had startled her. Caught up in her thoughts, she did not see the man watching her every move behind her. Walking briskly into Henry's room, she was startled to a stop when she saw someone standing beside the bed. A woman. Watching her lean down and kiss him, Jelissa started to back out of the room, when the woman turned.

There were tears running down her cheeks, shooting directly to Jelissa's heart. "Oh, I am so sorry, I did not realize he was having visitors," Jelissa said.

"I saw the news, and when he did not come for three days and I had not heard from him, I got worried. I am so sorry, where are my manners? My name is Meredith Jeffreys, Henry's wife." On the word wife, Jelissa felt her heart break into multiple pieces. Glancing down and seeing the ring on her hand, Jelissa straightened. Deciding that it was a hideous ring suited to come from a hideous man, she turned on her professional mode. Now was not the time to break down.

"Henry Jeffreys. That is the patient's name? Thank you so much, I will need to get his chart updated. Does he have any allergies to medications or had any recent major surgeries?" Jelissa asked briskly, grabbing the chart from the bed.

Panic raced across the woman's face when faced with the question. "Oh, my goodness, we are recently married. I am not sure about allergies to medicines, he is never sick. As for surgeries, no, he has not had any surgeries. He has always been so healthy." She quickly reached up and swiped at her eyes with her hands, more tears flowing.

Jelissa's heart ached for this woman. Newly married to someone who was making moves on her. Deciding that she would keep it to herself and threaten him if he ever woke up,

Jelissa focused on the task at hand. "Here is a tissue, I am so sorry that you had to find out this way. When we did not know who he was, we had no way of contacting his next of kin. I will need to get insurance information for him as well as a copy of his ID and social security number. Would you be able to provide that information for me? Or will you need to run home to see if you can find his information there?"

Relief came over Meredith's face, "Yes, I will need to run home, but I would prefer to be here when he wakes. Would you be willing to let him know his wife stopped by if he wakes?"

"It would give me the greatest pleasure to do so," Jelissa replied enthusiastically. Meredith nodded her head and, leaning down once more, she placed a kiss on Henry's mouth before straightening and leaving the room. Jelissa finished checking Henry's vitals and then left the room. Her shift was over, she would have to call a taxi to get home.

Calling for a cab, she finished up the paperwork she needed to. Glancing down as her phone vibrated, she looked at the text she received, stating her ride was there.

Picking up her purse, she walked out the door. Stepping into the taxi, she gave him her address. Staring out the window, she did not pay attention to where they were going until they pulled up outside her apartment. Belatedly realizing that she would not need Joe to watch Mr. Tickles for her, she shot him a quick text and rescinded her request for information on Henry. Walking up her steps, she opened the door before turning and locking it. Walking directly to her bathroom, she turned on the shower. Mr. Tickles walked in and wound his way around her legs.

Picking him up, she cuddled her face against him before placing him on the toilet lid. Stripping, she threw her clothes on the floor and stepped into the shower. Tilting her head back, she let the water run down her back. When the sob wrenched through her body, she dropped to the floor of the shower and let the tears come.

Chapter 16

Her body felt bruised and broken, every joint ached, and she could not seem to get anyone to tell her where she was or why she was there. Men had come in when they thought she was unconscious and did things to her that made her extremely nauseous. Placing her body in positions and taking pictures of her. They had said something about increasing revenue, but she did not understand what they meant by it. She was so tired that she felt she could not even cry. When she heard the door open again, she did not even pay any attention to it. Suddenly, she was heaved up and over someone's shoulder and carried into the light. She grimaced against the light but was too exhausted to even make a sound. Closing her eyes, she swayed with the motion. The continual pressure on her stomach started to become too much, when she heard voices.

"Hey! Where are you going with her?" a voice called behind them.

The man carrying her heard this and gruffly responded, "I went in there for my turn and found her dead. I'm taking her out to the dump site before the smell gets overpowering. Unless you think there are men who want to use her." At that statement, he stopped and made like he was going to turn back around. Confused, she hung there not making a sound and doing her best to not breath.

"Nah, man, do what you have to. That shit's nasty. Did have a nice ass, though," the man replied.

The man carrying her reached up and squeezed, agreeing with the man before moving on. As he opened a door, he quickly dropped his hand back down to her thigh. Walking briskly, she started to feel nauseous again, when he stopped. She heard what sounded like a trunk opening and then she was dropped in. The trunk closed, and then she felt the car begin to sway as he drove. Closing her eyes in exhaustion, she allowed herself to be lulled to sleep.

Jelissa realized suddenly that she was shivering. The water cascading down her was no longer hot. Getting up slowly, she shut off the water before stepping out of the shower. Mr. Tickles sat meowing repeatedly until she picked him up. Snuggling him, she wrapped herself in her robe and grabbed a towel off the hook. Picking up her phone, she saw a few missed messages and missed calls. Wandering out of the bathroom, she headed towards the bedroom, when she noticed the state of her apartment.

She had been so depressed and upset when she had walked in that she had not even noticed that her home had been trashed. As far as she could tell, nothing had been stolen, but her couches had knife gouges in them and all her glass was broken. Walking down the hall, all the pictures she had on the walls had been torn from there and thrown to the ground. It was the holes in the wall that started worrying her, as she could feel the rage the person must have felt. Pulling out her phone, she called 911, hoping it would be someone she could trust who would show up. She pulled out her phone and started taking pictures of all the damage.

Wondering who would do this and why, she was startled when there was a knock on the door. Going to open it, she recognized Nate and the man, Ignoramus, who she had met at the hospital before. Nate had his pinched look on his face, which he had whenever he saw something distasteful. Difference was that he had not seen the damage yet, he was looking at her. She realized she was standing in her robe with the towel still on her hair. Standing up straighter, she showed them into the apartment.

"Looks like you have made some enemies, ma'am," Ignoramus drawled softly. Certain that she had misheard him, she looked at him, startled to see the glee on his face. "I warned you not to mess with people that you shouldn't. "I 'preciate you callin' while I was on duty to see this. Yer' not really 'spectin us to do 'nuthin 'bout this, right?" Incredulous, she looked to Nate before realizing that he could not show they knew each other. When Nate chuckled to what was said, she saw red and started to launch herself at him, when she saw his eyes fall on hers. Pulling herself back, she did not throw the punch she wanted to, knowing she would be booked.

"I was hoping you would, 'protect and serve,' as you're called to do. Or is that also above your pay grade?" Jelissa demurred. A gasp barely escaped her lips before she felt his hand at her throat squeezing roughly as he slammed her against the wall.

"You will watch your place. Do you understand me? I am not someone to fuck with, and you would do best to recognize that!" Ignoramus whispered fiercely. She was amazed at the clarity in which he spoke, more shocked by that than him pinning her to the wall. When his hand reached inside her robe, she was not expecting this and started to struggle. He gripped her neck harder, cutting off her air supply and making it difficult to fight back. His hand cupped her breast before squeezing and twisting until the pain brought tears to her eyes.

Running his hand down the side of her stomach, he started to reach between her legs, when Nate suddenly cleared his throat. Glancing behind him, Ignoramus shook his head in disgust before reaching up and smacking first Jelissa's abused breast and then her face. "Remember this, bitch. He may be here to stop me this time, but he won't be next time. You can count on it." Slamming her once more into the wall, knocking her head against it, he released her. She slid to the floor, waiting for the next level of abuse. When she finally caught her breath, she looked up to see that they were gone. No report was going to be filed. She looked out her windows, and when she saw how dark it was, she was momentarily stunned and confused. Looking down at her phone again, she saw that it was almost 6 o'clock. Time to start getting ready for work.

Pulling herself to her feet, she started to walk to the front door and shut it. Grimacing at the pain in her throat and on her breast, she walked slowly to her bedroom and started to get dressed. As she pulled on her scrub top, her phone rang.

Distractedly picking up her phone, she answered without looking at the display.

"Guess you didn't call your boyfriend off in time, did you?" the voice on the other side inquired.

Looking down at the display, she saw that the number simply said blocked. "He is not my boyfriend, what do you want from me?" Jelissa asked wearily. Hand going to her throat at the pain it took to speak.

"I want you to call off your pig."

"My pig? I don't understand. What are you talking about?" Jelissa was completely confused. She had not slept in over 24 hours and now this guy was playing word games.

"The kid with the blue jeep. You know who I am talking about. Call off the pig, or she dies. You know how this works. I tell you what I want, and unless you want to be responsible for your friend's death, you'll do as I say. Hopefully this isn't too difficult to understand and I won't need to find someone who can speak more your speed." There was a click on the other end of the line. Jelissa kicked the wall in frustration at once again being hung up on.

Texting Joe as she headed out her door, she asked that he call her as soon as possible. Locking and shutting her apartment door, she realized that she had completely neglected Mr. Tickles and would need to make it up to him. Deciding that she needed a nap, she ordered a car to take her to the hospital, hoping that she could rest on the drive. Then, she would use an on-call room to sleep as long as she could.

Still seeing that she had missed messages, she decided to check the text messages first. It was when she saw the picture of a woman with her legs open, lying naked on the floor that she turned and vomited in the grass next to the apartment entrance. Checking her phone, she saw that Joe had not even looked at her texts. Texting him that it was urgent that she see him, she glanced up and saw that the car had arrived for her. Putting her phone to her ear, she listened to her voicemails. The message that shook her the most was one from the hospital saying that Henry had woken up and was refusing to talk to anyone but her. The last message surprised her. It was Karen asking her if she would like to meet up with Nicole and if she had any way to contact Joe and Henry. Shooting a quick text to

Karen that she would call her back on her break, she laid her head back and tried to sleep.

Pulling up to the hospital, the driver saw that she was asleep and did not know what to do with her. He could see bruises forming on her neck and her face and wondered what had happened to her. When he put the car in park, Jelissa's eyes flew open.

She dashed from the car into the hospital, quickly clocking in and heading to Henry's room. Before she entered, she masked her features. Throwing back her shoulders, she walked into the room. Seeing that it was empty of anyone other than Henry, she walked to the end of the bed as she would any other patient. Reaching down to pick up his chart, she did not see him open his eyes and take in her face. Seeing the bruises on her neck and face, he grew angry and extremely alarmed. "My pet, what's wrong?"

Jelissa's face hardened at the nickname. "I have not given you leave to call me pet. You are never to call me pet, ever again. You are never to kiss me ever again. Or hold me or act like you care. Do you understand?" Jelissa ground out through gritted teeth. Henry looked at her with confusion, then hurt, on his face before shuttering his expression. "Now that I know you're awake," Jelissa added as she put away his chart and started to exit his room, "I will call your wife so that she can see you. She was crying her eyes out over you. Only, I don't know why."

"Jelissa, wait!" Henry called from his room. Ignoring him, Jelissa made her way to the front desk to call Meredith, hurting all over again that he had lied to her and used her this way. Glancing down at her phone, she saw that she still had not heard from Joe. Concerned, she decided that on her lunch she would give him a call. Faith had been right, she could trust Joe; she definitely could not trust Henry.

Something felt off to Joe and he could not decide what it was. Finishing up the paperwork he was working on, he quickly headed out of the sushi restaurant, loving that he could have a lunch whenever he needed at the front of his organization. Starting to head back to his house, he remembered that he needed to get the report for Nicole's house. Running back in, he placed a few calls to some of his connections asking that they get him the information as quickly as possible. He had also put the lab on figuring out who Henry was. There were a lot of possibilities, and they said it could take them a couple of days.

As he got to his jeep, he remembered that Hope had written him out a list of things that she wanted from the store. Pulling out of park, he pulled into traffic, heading towards the store. He also wanted to get her a cell phone so that she could call him in case of an emergency. He had already informed his supervisor that he would be based out of his home for the next couple of weeks. He had an asset he was providing protection for and did not feel comfortable leaving it alone. When pressed for more information, Joe had declined, saying he was not sure if they had a leak in their department. After seeing Nate, he wanted to be sure that he only gave information that was necessary to get the job done and would not give away more information than what was strictly necessary. Stopping to get his phone, he glanced at the list in his hand while waiting in line.

Grinning, he read down the list before realizing that he was heading to the wrong store. Figuring that she wanted something for clothes or toiletries, he had headed towards the mall. Now that he saw the list, he realized that he needed to head to a home improvement store instead. He was pleased that she seemed to be taking an interest in his home, laughing when she put a note on the end that she could pay him back for the materials. Seeing a simple phone that could make calls, he grabbed it, then grabbed a small tablet too. Something to keep her busy, since he did not have a TV at his house.

Finishing up his shopping at the home improvement store, he headed to his house. The unease he had been feeling all day pressed down on him even more. He had only been gone for a few hours, but something felt wrong. He would be happy when he could get Hope the phone, so that he could call her when something like this happened. He knew that once he saw her or heard her voice, he would feel better. Pulling up into the drive, he saw the front of the house, still feeling disgust and, surprisingly, embarrassment that he was having Hope live in such a place. Deciding that it was fine just so long as she was safe, he continued up the drive.

When he saw the front door wide open, panic started in his gut. Throwing himself out of his car before he had even put it in park, he rushed up the front steps to the front door, pulling his weapon. He saw that the jam was broken and it appeared that someone had kicked the door in. Moving steadily through the house, he called Hope's name. Knowing with instinct that he should not announce himself but also knowing that she was not going to be there. When the shot rang out outside, he felt his heart plummet. Calling for Athena as he ran for her room, he knew she would help him find Hope. It was when he saw Athena's door open that the fear became almost too much. Feeling his phone vibrate, he pulled it out wishing he could call Henry for backup. Seeing that it was Jelissa, he stashed away his phone and headed out the door. Running towards the trees, he suddenly heard sobs coming off to the left.

Moving as quickly as he could, he blended into the trees, the sound of Hope's sobs like a beacon to where she was. Hoping Athena was there to keep her safe, he moved along. Seeing three men standing over Hope, Joe almost lost his ability to stay in control. It was when he saw Athena that he resolved to kill every person who would dare hurt his woman and dog. Startled at his thought of Hope, Joe took in the scene, hoping to catch Hope's eye and take the men out.

The weight of the body on top of her knocked the air out of her and she trembled in fear. She heard a shot ring out in the trees and the sound of Athena yelping. Glancing up, she saw Athena mere feet from her, panting heavily. "No!" Hope yelled. "Leave her alone, she is only trying to protect me." A blow to the back of Hope's head stunned her. She saw Athena move to react. Hope quickly told her to stay. Whimpering, Athena lay back down, closing her eyes as her breathing became more labored. "Please, just let me help her. She did not do anything wrong."

Turning her head to the side, she tried to focus on the men standing around her. Unsure of what she could do now, but she had promised herself this morning that she would not stand by and let things happen to her anymore. When she felt a hand on her calf, she jumped, suddenly realizing that she had never gotten dressed after her shower. The only thing between her and the men was a flimsy bathrobe. Focusing on her surroundings, she tried to find a way to get out of the men's grasp. Noting in the back of her mind that the men were starting to talk lewdly about her, she ignored them as best she could, hoping to find a rock or a branch or something that she could fend them off with. In the recesses of her mind, she could feel hands tearing the robe from her body. The men forgot their surroundings as they all reached down to run their hands over Hope's body.

When she placed her hands beneath her to push herself up and get them off her, she felt a knee at the base of her neck holding her down. The hands on her body were pinching and pulling and covering every inch of her. The weight of one man on her legs and the knee on her neck inhibited her from moving at all. It was as she turned her head to the side, searching for the yellow door, that she saw movement in the trees. Focusing on it, she hoped it was a wild animal. Seeing Joe, she almost gasped in relief.

Eyes travelling to his face, she realized that she had gotten what she wished for. A wild animal. She could see the ferociousness in his eyes as he stared at the men. Catching her eye, she pressed her lips into a firm line, ready to deal with whatever she had to for Joe to be able to get the three men. When she heard the zipper come down, she stopped them with her voice. "Wait, let me help you with that. Please." At her request, the men stopped, turning her head, she looked at the man closest to her. Bringing her hands to his zipper, she slowly pulled it down, before pulling him free of his pants. Turning to the next, she signaled that she would like to help him as well. Taking her hand to his zipper, she felt the third man start to press between her legs.

Bile rose in her throat as she realized that she may have to let these men rape her so that they would be distracted enough for Joe to get to them. Meeting his eyes, she saw him tense as she touched the men. Disgust crossed his features. Ashamed, she blushed crimson red. Closing her eyes, she tried to withdraw.

"I bet that pretty little mouth could take care of me until it's my turn, what do you say, slut?" the man closest to her head said. Turning and catching his eye, she nodded her acquiescence before being hauled up on her hands and knees to better accommodate the men. Closing her eyes, she opened her mouth, when she heard a gunshot ring out and the man in front of her groaned and dropped in front of her. Two more shots rang out and the other two men fell.

Opening her eyes, she pushed her way past the men and ran to Athena. Joe pulled out his cell phone and called 911 as he watched her tend to Athena. Quickly pulling off his jacket, he put it around her shoulders, careful to not touch her. He was shaking in anger when he saw what those men had planned for Hope. It was the glint of a blade that made him decide to shoot. Unsure if they had planned to use it, he had not been willing to take that chance.

"Joe, she is still breathing, we need to get her to the vet. Please, we cannot lose her, she got shot trying to save my life." Joe quickly pulled out his phone again. Calling the veterinarian, he asked if she would be willing to come to his home to take care of Athena. Hope was using pieces of her torn robe to try to stop the bleeding. When Joe leaned down to help with Athena, he watched Hope flinch away from him. Walking around to the other side of Athena, he watched and listened as Hope cooed to her, encouraging Athena that she would be okay. At a loss for what to do, Joe started walking back towards the house.

"Joe, where are you going?" Hope asked, feeling the beginnings of panic.

Without even turning around or stopping, he replied, "Meeting the cops at the road."

Hope watched as he walked away. Looking down at herself, she realized how awful she must look. Grasping the sides of the jacket he had put on her, she pulled them closed, then laid down next to Athena. Closing her eyes, she decided that perhaps it would be best to simply disappear. He would not notice anyway. As the sound of his footsteps grew quieter, Hope slowly felt herself withdraw to the yellow door. As she reached for the door handle, she felt Athena move next to her, licking her face. Even in her discomfort, she was doing her best to keep Hope from being upset.

Rubbing her hand up and down her fur, she tried to give comfort while taking comfort. It was the sound of footsteps approaching that caused her to tense. Joe should not have been back to them yet, which meant that someone else was heading back towards them. She waited for Athena to tense as well. When she did not tense, Hope opened her eyes and looked at her. Seeing that her eyes were closed and her breathing was shallow, she closed her eyes and waited for the last breath, terrified and devastated that she was going to die because of her.

When hands reached down and lifted Athena up, she opened her eyes and saw Joe. "I am sorry I left. I shouldn't have done that. We need to have a conversation later about what happened today. But, for now, will you please walk with me? I know this is strange, but can you hold onto my jean pocket on the back of my pants?" Lifting Athena close to his chest, he started to walk away, when he felt Hope pull away. He watched as she picked up the tattered pieces of her robe, grimacing as she bent over. It was then when Joe saw the blood on her hands and feet. Her knees and legs were scratched and bleeding. Based on the way she was holding her ribs, she probably had one cracked as well. It was seeing her determination that made Joe stop and second-guess having the conversation with Hope.

Hope walked towards Joe and took ahold of the back pocket of his jeans. As they started trekking out of the forest, Hope calmly dropped small pieces of her robe, creating a path directly to the bodies of the men who had attacked them. Joe could hear her breathing heavily and then occasionally gasping in pain as she walked. At one point, she gasped and slipped, going down on her knee. Joe wanted to be able to help her, but the weight of Athena was becoming burdensome. "Are you…?"

"I'm fine. Please do not concern yourself with me. I will get there just fine. My mother always said I was quite stubborn," she huffed.

Joe gritted his teeth to her response, tired of being blown off every time he showed concern for her. He was disgusted with the way she had been treated, disgusted with the way that he had treated her, and now he was disgusted with the way she was treating herself. He was formulating a reply when he heard the sirens ahead. He felt Hope jerk and realized that she was terrified of who was coming. Catching her eye, he asked what he was terrified of asking before, "Are some officers people who have hurt you?"

"Yes."

Chapter 17

At the sound of the sirens, Hope first felt regret, because she knew that Joe had been about to say something, then all-consuming fear. She wanted to disappear, just fall into the earth and end up at her mother's cave and not have to deal with anything. It was Joe's question that grounded her, made her remember that there was someone on her side. At his question, she was succinct with her yes, feeling no need to prevaricate with her answer. It was the wild animal that entered his eyes again that sent a thrill down her spine. A feeling she did not recognize. Shaken from her thoughts, she saw the cars pull up in front of her and Joe just beyond the trees.

"Hey," Joe whispered to get Hope's attention. When she stared stricken at the cars beyond the line of trees to the men getting out, he tried again. "Little One, look at me!"

At his words, Hope stopped and looked at him, amazed at the name he had given her. Rather than feeling belittled she felt, safe, cared for, and, strangely, loved. She watched as Joe adjusted Athena in his arms and then reached out and cupped her cheek with his hand. "Stay strong for me, just a little while longer, Little One. No one else will lay a hand on you unless you want them to."

Speechless, Hope gently pressed her lips against his palm before situating herself behind Joe. "I'm ready," she said. Joe took a shuddering breath and started moving towards the edge of the trees. He felt a quick tug that stopped him in his tracks. He saw her drop the last scraps from her robe and pull the sides of his jacket tighter over her body. Unfortunately, it only enhanced her beauty. Before he could say something, they were spotted by the officers and they raced towards him while some stormed the house to clear it. Watching the men make their way towards them, Joe could hear Hope's breathing become faster and shallower.

"Little One, I will keep you safe, I promise you. Please, I need you to trust me. I know I haven't kept you safe up to this point, but I promise you that this will change. I just need you to stay strong for me a little longer. Okay?" Joe whispered urgently.

After taking multiple deep breaths, Hope felt a calm settle over her at his words. She would be okay, as long as she had Joe by her side. "Okay, Joe." As soon as the words left her mouth, they were surrounded by the officers. Questions started being launched at them from all sides. Burying her face into Joe's back, she ignored the probing stares and questions. She noticed that Joe kept walking and stayed with him. He walked calmly and determinedly straight to a white truck in the back. Walking up to the woman, he kissed her on the cheek. "You're an absolute angel."

Hope watched the exchange and did her very best to not become jealous. Watching the way that Joe looked at this woman, she could tell that he loved her very much. Realizing that she was ridiculous to have thought that Joe, or anyone, could look at her as more than a disgusting victim, she straightened her shoulders and stepped out from behind Joe. Reaching over to Athena's head, she pressed her forehead to Athena and whispered, "Stay strong for me, Athena, I cannot do this without you." Straightening, she watched as the woman placed Athena on the passenger seat of the car instead of on the bed of the truck as Hope was expecting. When she turned, Hope was stunned by her beauty and realized that she would need to leave Joe's house tonight.

Reaching out her hand to the woman, Hope introduced herself, "Hello, my name is Emilia, I would really appreciate it if you could take care of Athena for me. I got lost in the woods and she helped me. I am very grateful to her."

Joe turned to look at Hope, surprised by what she had said but not wanting to endanger the vet, he went along with it. "Emilia, this is my sister, Sandra. Sandra is the best veterinarian in the state and also the best sister in the world. She will take care of Athena like she is her own, because she practically is hers. Anytime I go on vacation, she is the one who takes care of her."

Sandra looked at Joe funny before turning to look at Hope. "Hello Emilia, it is nice to meet you. Not sure why about all the extra information, but I am sure you will understand why I need to take my leave. I need to get Athena taken care of. Excuse me and good luck." Reaching forward, she pulled first Joe into a strong hug, whispering something in his ear. Then, impulsively, she leaned forward and hugged Hope. As she pulled away, Hope heard, "Stay strong, Hope, and please trust Joe." Smiling, she hopped into the truck before taking off down the drive.

Joe turned questioning eyes towards Hope before turning to the officers that, by now, were impatiently waiting for him to start answering questions. It was when Hope stepped forward that he got extremely nervous. She opened her mouth to speak, when she suddenly collapsed on the ground next to Joe. He watched as multiple officers reached down to pick her up and he leapt in front of them. The thought of any of those men touching her disgusted him. The surge of protectiveness came suddenly and naturally. He pulled her into his arms and took her into the house. Asking the officers to wait downstairs, he informed them to find the three bodies, they could follow the scraps of fabric.

Rushing up the stairs, he kicked the men in his room out, slamming the door with his foot. He quickly laid her on the bed before covering her up. Brushing her hair from her face, he pressed a kiss to her forehead. As he straightened to pull away from her, he saw her eyes open. "I panicked. I did not know what to say. I know no one is supposed to know that I am here. So I did the only thing I could think of doing to keep them from asking questions: I pretended to faint. You were supposed to catch me. That's what they do in the movies, you know?" Smiling softly, she curled up on the pillow and closed her eyes.

Joe was astounded that she was smiling and closing her eyes with him near. Making his way to the door, he stopped, stepping back to the bed. "Hope, put this under the pillow with you. If anyone comes in without knocking seven times first, you shoot first, and we will ask questions later, okay?" Placing the gun from his waistband into her hand, he walked from the room without even waiting for her response. Firmly shutting the door, he made his way grimly down the stairs.

Hope lay in bed thinking about what had almost happened to her out there. She wondered why it was her and why people kept trying to find and attack her. Realizing that just by being there she had put Joe and Athena in danger made her angry and sad, all at the same time. The damage had already been done to Athena, and she did not know that she would ever be able to forgive herself for that. Her skin felt like it was crawling with bugs. Hating that she was lying in bed, she wanted to get up but could not seem to work up the strength to do so. Snuggling down in the pillow, she waited, hate starting to consume her body.

Getting Meredith's voicemail would have been easier for Jelissa. Knowing this, she was not surprised when she, in fact, had the phone picked up by Meredith. "Hello, Meredith speaking, can I help you?" she said briskly.

Slightly taken aback by the professional tone, Jelissa decided to use it as her model and do the same. "Hello, this is the nurse Jelissa from Plumeria Hospital in Oasis Glen."

"How can I help you ma'am?" Meredith reiterated.

"I am sorry, do I have the wrong number? I am looking for Henry's wife, Meredith. Is that not you?" Jelissa was starting to feel uneasy.

"Oh! Um! Yes! That is me! I am so sorry, I am just so terribly exhausted that I was not paying close enough attention. Is my love okay?" she breathlessly responded. Jelissa started to feel better, until she heard a man's voice in the background and Meredith's voice muffled. Realizing that she had her hand over her phone to cover the sound, Jelissa was reticent to provide any more information. Then realizing it might be her brother or dad, and, also, none of Jelissa's business, she quickly started speaking.

"Yes, Mrs. Jeffreys, Henry has woken up and cannot stop asking for you. You requested I call you as soon as he woke, and he has. Should I tell him to expect you?"

"Oh, I will do my very best to get over there tonight, but I have work and so I may not get there until morning. Could you pass him a message for me, though? It may seem quite out of the ordinary, but it's a little inside joke for us. Would you mind?" Without bothering to wait for consent, she continued. "Will you just tell him that the coffee was very hot this morning and I almost burned my tongue but managed to cool it down first? I really appreciate it. I have to run, but please give my, um, muffin, all the best from me." With that, she hung up the phone. Jelissa was so at a loss for words that she simply sat with the phone in her hand for a moment before placing it back on the cradle.

Taking a deep breath, she started to get up to go back to Henry's room when she heard a crash and saw Henry standing outside his room pulling his stand for his IV bag, making his way towards her. Rolling her eyes, she moved quickly towards him, snagging a wheelchair on the way. When she got to him, she put the brakes on and helped to lift him into the chair. Gasping when his shoulder hit her breast, having forgotten the damage done by Ignoramus. When Henry was positioned in the wheelchair, Jelissa started pushing him back to his room.

"My pet, I'm sorry. Jelissa, please tell me what happened. We had a wonderful time tonight, why are you so short with me now? I can explain about Meredith," he began. As they turned to go into the room, Jelissa rammed his leg into the door frame, before quickly correcting it and shoving him in the room.

"Oh, oops, sorry. Hope that didn't hurt. I get so clumsy sometimes when I work. Surely you understand how mistakes can happen. Kind of like our date," Jelissa said snidely.

Coming around the chair, she started to help him from the chair, when she saw the pain on his face. Immediately contrite, she knelt before him. Dropping her gaze, she tried to take a breath that would not hurt so much and would calm her. Even if she did not like Henry, she did need to remember that she was a nurse and not someone who should cause her patient any pain. When he put his knuckles below her chin and lifted her eyes, they were both surprised by the tears he found on her cheeks.

"My pet, she is not my wife. She is my partner from work. I promise there is no other, and I do not want another." Lifting her face to his, he placed a gentle kiss on her lips before withdrawing and putting his forehead against hers.

Jelissa took a shuddering breath when she realized how much that fit with how the woman had acted. Ashamed by her jealousy and embarrassed, she was stunned when he kissed her and told her he did not want another. "I was so scared for you. To walk in and see this other woman crying over you and kissing you, it hurt so bad. I wanted to be that woman, and when I realized that the role was already taken by someone else, I was so devastated." Pulling away from his forehead, she helped lift him enough to stand and get into his bed. When he started to, instead, walk towards the couch, she helped him walk over. He sat and tugged her down next to him before tucking her against his chest.

"The date, it wasn't tonight, was it? Our job has a protocol to not go looking until three days, minimum, have passed. How long have I been out?" Henry gently prodded.

"Tonight was your fourth night. I've been so terrified. I am glad you're awake. I hate that you were hurt. I do not understand why you left me to go to Nicole. I have a feeling it was because you knew she had been abducted or you had been told to check on her." He started to speak and she shook her head. "Not tonight." Snuggling in closer to him, she relaxed into his arms. Realizing that she had so much to tell him and how exhausted she was, she gave up any pretense of being able to function and started to fall asleep against him. Before she completely fell asleep, she whispered, "I love you, Henry."

Certain that he had not heard her properly but hoping he had, he snuggled her closer. He was terrified for her. He could see the bruises on her neck and face and recognized that they were placed there by someone who had tried to hurt her. That she had not told him what had happened concerned him, however, he knew there was a lot of trust to be reestablished. He also wondered if Meredith had left a message for him. When he went to ask her, he felt her fully relax into him and fall asleep. Gently, he placed a kiss against the crown of her head and lay his head atop hers.

The lull of the car swaying back and forth pushed the woman into oblivion. She was startled awake by the car stopping and the trunk being thrown open. When she was lifted from the car, she was surprised when she was cradled in the man's arms instead of being thrown over his shoulder. The moon was bright overhead and cast an eerie glow all over his face. When she tried to look at him, he gently hushed her and told her to rest. Soothed by his words, she slowly leaned her head against his chest.

He seemed to be walking into a house through the garage that he had pulled into. As he walked, the lights turned on. There was a beeping that seemed to be getting louder as he walked. He bent down and pressed some buttons on a panel before appearing to rearm it. As he walked down the hallway, she tried to take in her surroundings, but the lights were far too bright for her eyes. He groaned a little when she rotated against him. Concerned, she looked at him, worried that she had hurt him.

"I am sorry. I just realized that you may not have the strength to bathe yourself," he said as he walked into the bathroom. "Would you like to try? Or at least soak? I will only put a little in there, if you'd prefer." He looked so panic-stricken, but the idea of a bath sounded amazing. She tried to lift herself up from his shoulder but could not.

"Um, I don't have to bathe. I can just sleep on the floor or something. It will feel almost like home," she grimaced at her attempt at a joke. Numb to her nudity, she thought of all the ways that she had been used in the last…she did not even know how long. "How long? How long was I in that place?" she asked.

The man hung his head, "Seven days. I am sorry it took me so long to get you out. But I could not seem to make it in successfully without being seen. When I came in tonight, I really thought you were dead, so it seemed the perfect reason to take you out."

Squinting her eyes, she focused on the face of the man who had taken her from that hellhole. She gasped when she recognized him. Eyes widening, she felt nausea start to rise in her. He moved quickly, opening the toilet seat and lowering her down next to it. Clinging to it, she vomited bile and blood into the toilet before dry-heaving multiple times. He quickly ran water in the sink and placed a wet cloth against her neck before slowly bringing it around to her face. Wiping the vomit and filth from her face, he gently leaned her against the wall. Closing the toilet lid, he flushed. He turned to turn on the bath when he heard his doorbell chime. "Ah, good. Right on time. I will be right back. I am afraid I do not have bubbles. Please do not go anywhere."

He quickly turned on the bath and adjusted the temperature after testing it with his hand. Grabbing another towel from the counter, he quickly wiped his hands as he walked towards the front door. Sitting in the bathroom against the wall, she thought about trying to get away and realized how tired and thirsty she was. She heard another woman's voice and was worried he was going to hurt her. She remembered him as the man who had stood and watched while other men had defiled her.

The voices grew closer and she tried to sit up closer to the wall to prepare herself for whatever and whomever was going to come through that door. As the man walked in, she heard him chuckle softly. A woman came in the bathroom with him and immediately bit her lip before dropping down in front of her. She had beautiful porcelain skin and long blonde hair. Inquisitive and intelligent green eyes stared back at her, reminding her of the girl that had disappeared from the brothel one night.

"Hello, young lady, my name is Nicole, I am a nurse and I am here to help you. Let's get you washed up."

Chapter 18

Hope could hear the voices downstairs and wondered how long Joe could keep them from bothering her. She was surprised when, after only about 15 minutes, she heard the last footsteps descend the deck. Expecting to hear Joe coming back up the stairs to the room, she started to get nervous when everything fell silent downstairs. Getting up, she slipped on the sweatpants on the end of the bed and crept down the stairs. She had gotten very adept at missing the creaks. Grabbing her ribs as she walked down the stairs, the pain almost unbearable, she came to a halt at the end of the stairwell.

She could hear someone in the kitchen and wondered if it was Joe or someone else. Wishing she had Athena by her side, she crept to the door and peeked in. What she found broke her heart. Sitting at the counter on a bar stool, she found Joe with his head in his palms. The scene so similar to the one from the last day she had with her mom; she did not know what to do. Should she try to comfort him or let him be? Walking as quietly as she could into the kitchen, the sound of her feet padding on the floor alerted Joe to her presence. She watched his back straighten. "Please give me a couple minutes, Hope. I will be up to start your bath in a minute. I'll grab you the tea you probably want too. But right now, I need you to let me be," his voice broke at the end of the sentence.

Hope's heart broke at his words. Still torn, she took a step closer to him, when his words lashed across the room. "Would you just listen for once! Stop being so selfish and expect everyone to just cater to you. I asked you to leave me alone. Get out!"

Gasping, Hope turned and left the room. Going to his room, she grabbed the shopping bags that had carried her clothes.

Rushing to the wardrobe, she started throwing the clothes into the bags. Starting to leave the room, she realized that she still had Joe's sweatpants on. Ripping them from her body, she threw them on the bed before trying to pull on a pair of jeans. Grimacing in pain, she tried pulling on shoes and could not get them on with all the cuts to her feet. Going to the bathroom, she saw herself in the mirror. Seeing the dirt and leaves in her hair and on her face, she turned on the shower. Pulling the clothes off that she had just put on, she hopped quickly into the shower. She watched as the leaves and dirt flowed off her body and down to the drain. Jumping out of the shower, she did not bother clearing the drain. Pulling her clothes back on quickly, she took one last look around the room. Ripping the pages with descriptions of the people who had hurt her in the brothel out of her book, she left them on the bed.

Grabbing a pen, she scribbled down one last note before placing it on top of the stack of papers. Turning around one last time, she took her final glance of the room around her. Making her way quickly down the stairs, she left through the back door. Not bothering to even shut it, she took off towards the woods. Going in the opposite direction she had that morning. When she got to the tree-line, she turned back, "Thank you for everything and I am so sorry." Turning back to the woods, she entered the tree-line, quickly losing sight of the house.

Jelissa woke with pain in her neck from the awkward position she had fallen asleep in. She noticed that she was covered in a blanket and wondered who had come in and not woken her. Henry was asleep, breathing softly, leaning against her. She wondered how she could extricate herself from his arms without waking him. As she started to move, his arms immediately tightened around her. Thinking it was just a response in his sleep, she was startled by his voice. "Where are you going, uh, Jelissa?" he hesitated at her name. Pain evident in his tone on her name.

Jelissa sat silent for a moment, uncertain how to respond. Feeling embarrassed by the way she had responded to him and yelled at him about Meredith, she wanted to be able to take that moment away. However, the pain she had felt was so raw and so true that it was better that he knew how much she had been hurting at the thought of him being with someone else. Taking a bolstering breath, she responded, "I am technically supposed to be working. I was going to get up but did not mean to wake you." His arms tightened around her again and she leaned back into his chest. The pounding of his heart next to her ear calming her more than she thought possible.

"A nurse came in here, shortly after you fell asleep. When she couldn't find me, she started to panic. When she saw us over here, she came over, prepared to wake you, when she saw the extent of the damage on your face and neck. She asked me what had happened. Do you know how awful it was to not be able to say what had happened to you?" Anger and disappointment evident in his tone, he continued, "She went to get a doctor, who came back. Based on the damage that he could see without waking you, he wanted to wake you, I told him no, so he decided to call in another nurse. You have the rest of the night off. The rest of the nurses came together and covered your shifts for the next three days, actually. Apparently, you're extremely loved here, though that does not surprise me. You're extremely easy to love."

At his words, Jelissa suddenly remembered telling him that she loved him. Pushing up from the couch to look at him, she grew wary. "You do not have to say it back. I was tired and probably did not know what I was even saying. It had been a long night..." Henry placed his finger against Jelissa's lips, stopping her words.

"Jelissa, I think we need to start over and set some ground rules. The first and most important one is no lying, under any circumstances, no matter how big or how small. We are completely open about how we feel, what we think, and what our goals and dreams are. Do you think you would be willing to do that with me?" Henry held his breath, waiting for the answer. He had a lot of explaining to do, and he was prepared to do it, just as long as she was.

Jelissa got up from the couch, the need to go back to his touch so strong that she was almost breathless as she walked back and forth in front of him. Stopping, she turned to look at him, "Before I answer that, there is something that I need to do first." Henry dropped his glance, the disappointment so overwhelming. When he felt the couch dip next to him, he turned to see what she was planning. "Kiss me, please. Kiss me like you may never…" Henry cut off her words, placing his mouth on hers. There was nothing gentle about the kiss. He was branding her as his. His lips were punishing on hers as he pressed her into the couch. The pain in his ribs to the point of being unbearable.

When he finally pulled away, they were both very short of breath. Gasping, he leaned forward and placed a gentler kiss on her lips before cradling her cheek. When they both caught their breath, Jelissa started to speak, when Henry once more plunged his hand into her hair. Dragging her head back, he plundered her mouth with his, before leaving her mouth to go to her neck, nipping as he went to her shoulder. When she placed her hands on his shoulders to steady herself, the pain from the burns became unbearable and he pulled back, grunting from the sharp pain.

"I do love you, Henry," Jelissa whispered, still gasping for breath. She could see that he was in pain and wanted to get something to help with it, but she wanted to make sure first that he understood how she felt. Leaning forward, she gently placed her lips to his before standing up to go grab pain medicine. He grabbed her hand, concern evident on his face. "I am just going to get you some medicine. I know how much pain you're in." Moving to the call button on the bed, she paged another nurse, requesting the medicine. Turning back towards Henry, she once again found herself at the full attention of a man, much as she had that first day in the café with him.

Thinking back on the few weeks they had had together, she suddenly remembered Meredith and her message. Realizing that she had so much to tell him, she sat down next to him and started speaking rapidly, telling him about what had happened with Nicole and what Meredith had said. At her words, he straightened up. "Wait, is that what she said or is that a derivative of what was said? This is important, Jelissa!" Henry interrupted. Seeing the concern and frustration on his face, she closed her eyes to remember what exactly Meredith had said.

Henry mistook her closing her eyes as being hurt and shook himself from his frustration. It was not like him to forget his place so quickly. She still did not know what he did. They had a lot of catching up to do. However, knowing what the message was held very significant importance. Taking a calming breath, he leaned forward and placed a kiss gently on her lips. When he leaned back, a wry grin went over Jelissa's face. "I am not going to be able to focus if you keep doing that."

Henry pulled away slightly before leaning his forehead against Jelissa's. Waiting patiently, she relayed the message word for word as Meredith had told her. When she felt Henry pull away, she opened her eyes. The hardened face she saw on him scared her. "You don't work for the same company that Joe does, do you?" Henry's eyes met hers before hardening even further. A nurse entered the room, walking quickly to his IV. The halt in conversation pulling on both of them. When the nurse left the room, Henry finally answered.

"No, I don't. Unfortunately, our acquaintance must now come to an end. I have appreciated our time together, however, it just isn't feasible anymore at this time. Please grab me what I need to discharge myself. I understand it will be against the doctor's wishes, but I cannot stay here any longer." Waiting for the rage to start in Jelissa, he was staggered when she leaned forward and placed a kiss on his cheek.

"Thank you, also, for the time we have spent together. Take care of what you need to and stay safe." Rising slowly, she got to the door before she stopped and turned. "When you're ready to hold up your end of the bargain, you know where to find me." Walking from the room, she walked to the nurse's station, letting them know what Henry had requested. Double-checking her schedule and seeing that she did, in fact, have the next few days off, she decided to go home and start the long process of cleanup.

She realized, as she walked out of the hospital, that she had not told Henry about Joe and had not even had the opportunity to tell him what had happened with the officers and how she had come by the bruises on her face and neck. Straightening her shoulders, she started to call for a taxi when she realized that she had all the time in the world to get home. Turning, she headed down the sidewalk to take the long walk home.

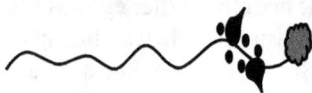

Karen pulled up to the hospital shortly after Jelissa left. She was concerned after not hearing any response from Jelissa or Nicole and decided it was time to 'grow a pair,' as her son had started saying, and just show up. Anxiety filled her as she parked her car and started to head up to the entrance. When she stepped on the curb and glanced up, she saw Henry being wheeled to the front door. Seeing that he was injured, she realized this might be why she had not heard from Jelissa. However, it did not account for Nicole's silence. Walking briskly up to him, still not sure she could trust him, she caught the devastation in his face.

"Henry, is everything okay?" Karen asked as she approached. The change that came over Henry at her question astounded her. Hardness entered his eyes and his unflinching gaze landed on hers.

"I don't know you. Why are you talking to me?" Henry snarled in response.

Taken aback, Karen started to just walk away, then was so overcome with anger that she, instead, leaned forward, placing her hands on either side of him on the wheelchair arms. "I don't know who you think you are, but you don't scare me and you won't intimidate me. Are Jelissa and Nicole okay? What have you done to them?" The last question slipped unbidden from her mouth. Momentarily stunned by the question, she was not prepared for Henry to stand and shove her back.

"I said I do not know you, woman! Get yourself away from me!" A black sedan with tinted windows pulled up to the curb at his words. "I don't know who you think I am, but you have the wrong guy. Now back off!" Limping slowly to the car, he reached for the passenger door's handle. The window lowered by a fraction and he appeared to be directed to get into the back seat instead. Straightening his shoulders, he pulled open the back door. Climbing in, the car pulled away before he even had time to close the door or buckle his seatbelt. The last thing Karen saw as the car pulled away was Henry looking at her with sorrow and regret on his face, pain on the edges.

She briskly walked into the hospital now, scared for Nicole and Jelissa. When she inquired at the nurses' station for the women, she was told that Jelissa had been given the next few days off and they could not release her address to her and that Nicole was no longer employed. At a loss, she left a note with the nurse for Jelissa to call her back as soon as possible. Hastily making her way back to her car, she pulled out her cell phone to call Jelissa, praying she would answer the call.

After helping the woman climb into the bathtub, Nicole headed out to her car quickly to grab some clothes that she hoped would fit the girl. Grabbing her medical bag, she briskly made her way into the house. Seeing the man at the door when she reached the porch, she slowly entered as he closed the door behind her. "Thank you," she murmured softly. She had only been to his house on one other occasion: when she had followed him trying to get information out of him.

She knew the location of the brothel and had multiple pictures of the men who frequented the location. The only problem: it was housed above a very prestigious nightclub. A place even she had frequented. It was difficult to know if the men went in for nefarious reasons. She had followed this man home after seeing him enter the facility too many times. A man on an officer's salary should not have been able to visit as often as he had, and he always went in alone and came back out after 30 minutes to an hour. She had not seen him go into his house and circle around her car. She had been sitting there when, suddenly, her car door had been yanked open and a pillowcase had been thrown over her head. He had dragged her into his house. Later ripping the pillowcase off her head, she had seen two wine glasses and a bottle of red and a bottle of white out on the counter.

147

She came to find out that he was an officer infiltrating the brothel as best he could while maintaining himself as a cop. That night had been particularly rough and he needed to wind down. It was that night when this woman, who was now in the bathtub, had been brought in and raped for the first time. To show his loyalty to the brothel, he had been forced to watch as she had been raped. He made it his goal to get her out as soon as he could. Nicole had sat and listened to his story before recognizing him.

He was the man who had called and left the door open at the brothel when she had been taken there. She had been drugged and barely made it away. She had woken more than a day later in the doorway of an abandoned building. Amazed she was still alive, she had slowly made her way home. Sneaking into her home, she had packed as many things from her house as she could. Hearing movement, she stealthily left through the front door, not bothering to lock it. The next morning, she saw on the news that her house had been engulfed in flames. Saddened and angered, she decided that she would do everything in her power to make the people who were trying to hurt her pay.

She had spent the night with Nate with him spilling everything that he knew about the brothel and who worked in it and who frequented it. After he had spilled all the information, she expected him to have to kill her. Instead, he had offered her his spare bedroom and shower. She had initially declined, until he had simply walked from the room to go to his own. She heard him lock the door and turn on the shower. It was the sound of his cursing and screaming in the shower that convinced her to stay. She had left a note on the counter in the morning next to freshly-baked muffins with her number. Thinking that she would be leaving before he got up, she was amazed to see that he had already left for the day.

Watching him now, she made her way slowly back to the bathroom. As she passed by him, she was stopped by his hand on her arm. "Thank you for coming," he said.

"Thank you for calling me," she simply replied before walking further into the home. It was time to get to work, and seeing the broken and battered woman in the bathtub, she was determined this woman would be different than Hope.

Chapter 19

The young woman in the bathtub had heard their exchange and wondered at their relationship. Opening her eyes at the sound of the bathroom door opening, she sank down under the water. The drugs she had been administered for the past week were starting to fade and she was aghast at her nudity. Looking down at her body, she could see nothing but bruises and cuts encompassing her entire body. The water had gone absolutely filthy, lending to a somewhat muted vision of her body under the water. She looked up and saw the woman, Nicole, sitting on the counter staring at her hands. Ashamed, she sank even further under the water, wishing her body could be completely hidden from view.

Closing her eyes, she wished she could just disappear. The shame she felt and the guilt were becoming extremely overwhelming. It was at the voice of Nicole telling her to 'Let it out' that she realized that tears were streaming down her face. Pulling her knees up to her chest, she dropped her head to her knees, sobbing uncontrollably. She wished she could forget everything. "Can we call my parents, please? I need them to pick me up."

Nicole's heart broke at the girl's words. She was going to need the support of her parents through this. However, based off the missing person's report, her parents were not even the ones who had reported her missing. Wondering what kind of people would not even notice that their own daughter was missing, she promised her she could call when she got out of the bath.

"So, like I mentioned earlier, I am a nurse. Would you object to me helping you bathe?" Nicole asked gently.

The woman looked at her with trepidation in her gaze. She mutely nodded her head before closing her eyes and lying back against the tub. Nicole started with her hair. It was full of spittle and semen and made her want to gag. The blood matting her hair was barely discernible. Interrupted in her thoughts, Nicole heard the young woman speak.

"Could you maybe talk, just so it's not so quiet? I need to not be thinking about the things done to me for the past week. I can keep hearing them call me a 'cum-slut'," she whispered.

"What is your name, sweetheart?" Nicole questioned.

"Lilliana, my friends call me Lilly," she answered, some of the tension leaving her shoulders. With her name, Nicole confirmed that she had correctly paired her with the missing person report.

"You remind me a bit of a woman I met a few weeks ago. Strong, beautiful, and someone who will survive this. I believe that her favorite color is yellow. So bright and so cheerful. What is your favorite color?" Lathering her hair in shampoo for the fourth time, she stepped back to text Nate. At the sight of the cell phone, Lilly got extremely nervous.

"Why are you getting out your cellphone?" she asked desperately.

Nicole cursed herself under her breath before responding. "I am texting Nate your name so he can contact your parents. I am sorry I didn't warn you before I got out my phone. Nate told me what they made him do. I am sure you are quite wary of phones now."

After receiving an affirmative response from Nate that he would contact her parents, Nicole reached into her bag to pull out her comb. Washing it quickly in the sink, she turned to see Lilly shivering.

"May I drain the tub and refill it with clean, warm water?" Nicole asked as she set down her phone. Surprised, Lilly nodded her head in agreement. Nicole reached down and lifted the plug before going up to her head. Not bothering to rinse the shampoo from her hair, she started to comb the shampoo-laden hair to rid it of knots. As she combed, she started noticing the similarities between her and Lilly. Long blonde hair with strands of darker brown. Many people called her hair dirty blonde. She preferred to call it honey. She was more slender, or lithe, than most people, especially with her height. There was a smattering of freckles across her nose and shoulders, just as there were for Nicole. Both had slender fingers—made for playing a piano, her mother used to say. Something that she never did. She wondered if Lilly did. Shivering despite not being cold, Nicole continued with her ministrations. The knock on the door jolted her and Lilly.

"One second," she called. Reaching over, she closed the curtain and plugged the drain, starting a new bath with a lot warmer water. After making sure that it was to Lilly's comfort, she left the comb beside the tub and stood to open the door. Not seeing anyone there, she told Lilliana she would be right back before closing the door behind her.

When she entered the bedroom attached to the bathroom, she saw Nate pacing back and forth, absolutely fuming with anger. Turning and seeing Nicole, he exploded, "They should be shot!"

Nicole rose her hands to placate him. "How about you start at the beginning and tell me what's wrong."

"I called those fuckers and asked if they were her parents. They said they didn't want her back. They said selling her was the best investment they had ever made. They are on vacation and won't be back for a couple weeks. Her own fucking parents sold her to those people. Apparently, they have availed themselves the services the brothel offers, as well. They like young ones. They said the 12-year-old was the best they've had. I've seen these people and I'm disgusted. What in the hell do we tell her?" he fumed.

At the sob, both Nicole and Nate turned to see Lilly standing in the doorway between the bedroom and bathroom, the heartbreak on her face gut-wrenching. She collapsed to the floor, overcome with the betrayal from her parents. Nicole turned to Nate and saw the self-disgust. He felt he had contributed to this. He had not been able to help her. He had not even been able to help Hope. Nate knew now that she had gotten out but had ended up shot in the hospital anyway by one of the chief's subs. With a cry of anguish and self-hatred, he stormed from the room, slamming the door on his way out. A picture on the wall of a plumeria fell to the floor, its glass shattering.

It was the sound of the glass shattering that snapped Lilly's head up. Seeing it, and seeing that Nate was gone, her face went pale. "Is he going to send me back?" she whispered desperately.

Nicole tried to maintain her patience, but it snapped with the question. "Are you kidding me? How much of that conversation did you hear? How much of that conversation did you see the devastation on his face? He is disgusted by the people who raised you. I won't even give them the benefit of calling them parents. They no longer get that title. He was devastated by what happened to you; he endangered himself to get you out. We have all had to do things we are ashamed and not proud of. Don't for one second think that he would ever voluntarily hurt you." Chest heaving with her response, Nicole headed towards the bathroom.

Lilly's face had gained color through the speech and now had anger radiating from her face. "How dare you act like you can speak to me that way? I have been raped in every orifice in my body. I've been beaten until I could not see. Did you not notice the bruises and scrapes encompassing my entire body? Did you forget that I have had my body violated in ways that would make you vomit profusely over and over? I did that! I vomited when they were violating me; you know what they did? They shoved my face in it until I couldn't breathe. The only way to breathe was to inhale it and eat my own vomit. So don't stand there and be self-righteous on me when you have no fucking clue what I have been through."

"And there is my girl. That is the fire I wanted to see. Those people who sold you, they will get what is coming to them. But the only way that is going to happen is if you fight back. Cry, rage, scream! I don't care what you do, but do not ever sit there like that again and look so broken." As Nicole spoke, she moved to the doorway, adding more warm water to the tub. Turning, she pointed to the tub, "Get in, we aren't done with you yet."

Startled and intrigued, Lilly made her way slowly back to the bathtub. As she climbed in, she calmly said, "Blue, my favorite color is blue."

Jelissa could not remember the last time she had walked for the sake of nothing to do. She was in decent shape from running from one end of the hospital to the other, however, that was all work. Today, this was not running, except it was. She was running away from Henry and what he had just done to her. The constant ups and downs had become too much. She had watched the change come over his face with the message delivered from Meredith. Where she had expected to be defeated and broken with his rejection, she instead felt liberated.

Even with the rejection, the love in his eyes, it was still there. She knew he had not said it yet, however, he had wanted to. There was no doubt that he felt the same way. When she had told him that she would be waiting, the hope that had flared in his eyes was enough for her. She made her way home slowly. At the slight buzzing sound, she looked around for a bumblebee, wanting to see it. Reaching into her pocket to snag her phone to snap a picture, she realized that it was her phone creating the noise. Seeing Karen's name on the display, she took a deep breath before answering.

"Hey Karen, it's good to finally hear from you," Jelissa answered as cheerily as she could.

"Jelissa, I am so glad you are okay, I just left from the hospital and saw Henry. Are you okay? Did he hurt you? What's going on? Where is Nicole? Have you heard from Joe?" Karen babbled quickly.

"Hey, let me give you my address, come over for dinner around 5:30, if you can. I will be happy to answer all your questions then. I may even see if Joe can show up, as, yes, I have been in touch with him." Waiting until Karen confirmed that she could come to her place, she gave her the address and hung up. Pulling her phone back out, she started to text Joe when she realized that he did not respond to her other texts. Deliberating between texting him again or calling him, she was startled when her phone buzzed again. Seeing a text, she was hopeful that it was Joe. When she saw Nicole's name pop up, she braced herself for what the picture would be.

Opening the text, she saw a picture of Nicole slung over a guy's shoulder, completely naked. The caption read, 'Too late. She's dead. Which friend do we choose next?'

Hanging her head, she took a deep breath as tears started coursing down her cheeks. Placing her phone back in her pocket, she started heading home. Her heart taking a volatile turn as she realized that she might need to sacrifice herself so that she would not have any other friends taken. She heard her phone buzz again and decided to ignore it this time. She just could not take it. Not today. Noticing that it was getting dark, she lifted her head and saw that clouds were rolling in. The air grew crisp. It was the beginning of November, so rain was not unheard of. However, in Oasis Glen, they rarely started feeling cooler weather until closer to Christmas.

The wind picked up before thunder rocked across the sky. Concerned, as she had never seen the weather change so rapidly, she increased her pace hoping she could beat the storm home. Lightning streaked across the sky. Seeing this, she grew even more worried and went into a jog. She was not sure she was going to be able to make it to her apartment in time.

It was the sound of thunder that made Joe raise his head from his hands. He had heard the back door slam some time earlier but had not thought anything of it. Figuring Hope needed to be alone, he had not gone after her. Hearing the thunder, though, he realized that it was time to get her inside. Stepping over to the stove, he lit the fire under the tea kettle before sloshing it to check for water. Seeing that it was empty, he leaned over and picked it up, taking it to the sink to fill. Glancing out the window over the sink, he saw lightning streak across the sky. Knowing that this was abnormal, he grew concerned that it might be more than just a simple storm. Quickly placing the tea kettle on the stove, he made his way to the hallway.

Seeing the back door was still open and realizing that it was the screen that had slammed earlier, he was a bit miffed that she had not bothered to close the door. He had the heater running and did not want to heat the outside, or cool it in the summer, simply because she was too annoyed to take care of closing the door. Stepping out on the deck, he was a bit surprised to not see her there. Calling her name, he grew even more annoyed when she did not answer. Turning around, he closed the door and screen before heading up the stairs. Thunder shook the house as he made his way up the stairs. Upon reaching the top, he went straight to their bedroom. At his thoughts on 'their', he stumbled a bit, before resuming heading to his bedroom.

By the time he reached his doorway, he was livid that she was acting so spoiled with this situation. When he walked into the room, he immediately felt that something was different, something was off. A feeling of emptiness swept over him. Seeing the wardrobe doors open and many of her clothes missing, he prayed she had simply moved to a different room. However, he knew in his gut that she was gone. Starting to back out of the room, he saw some paper on the bed. Rapidly making his way to the bed, he picked up the papers, seeing descriptions of people, some of whom he knew. What caught his breath at the note she had left, simple and yet so poignant, was:

You were right. I am selfish. I am sorry. Goodbye.
–Hope

Racing from room to room, he relived how he had felt when he had gotten home earlier that afternoon. Realizing that it had been less than five hours since he had searched for her last, he realized what he had done. She was terrified and broken. She had allowed her body to be touched in order for him to take care of the men who had attacked her. She had lied to his sister to not endanger her. She had pleaded for Athena's life. Without her there to apply pressure on Athena's wounds, there was a strong possibility that she would have been dead already. Realizing that he had not told her that his sister had called and said that Athena was stable, he ran his hands through his hair, ashamed of how he had handled everything. He had promised to keep her safe. Yet, when she had tried to give him comfort, he had shunned her and pushed her away.

He made his way slowly down the stairs, deliberating if he should bother going after her. There was no way he would know where she went. As he had told her just that morning, there were over 100 acres out there. Easy to get lost or, in this case, easy to hide in. He suddenly heard a scream come from the kitchen. Heart racing, he thundered down the stairs. Before he reached the kitchen, the screaming stopped. Pulling the weapon on his belt, he turned the corner, astounded when he saw Hope standing there, tea kettle in hand. Belatedly, he realized that the scream was the tea kettle.

She glanced at his gun, then back to his face, completely unflinching. Turning, she poured herself a cup. When thunder shook the house, she shrank within herself, then straightened. Going to sit at the bar, she did not even offer a cup to Joe. Placing the mug on the bar, she turned back around before pouring a mug of hot coffee into a glass. Pouring some cream into the coffee and adding a single spoon of pure, raw sugar, she slowly stirred before bringing it to his spot. Before placing it down, she slowly brought it to her lips and took a quick sip. Turning, she went back to the refrigerator and added a little more cream. Once more bringing it to her lips, she nodded her head in satisfaction before placing his mug on the counter.

Joe stood in the kitchen, a riot of emotions going over his face. His heart was pounding in his chest. He realized, standing there watching her, that his feelings were running deeper than he had realized. It was because of those feelings that he had not wanted to feel weak. Taking a step towards the bar, he surprised both himself and Hope when he simply sat and placed the gun on the counter. Picking up his mug, he brought it to his lips. When he took a sip, he was amazed at the explosion of flavor on his tongue. She had made it perfectly. Bemused, he realized that she paid much more attention than he had ever realized. He had so much to say, and there was so little that he knew he could tell her. He knew she had left, that was clear by the state of the wardrobe and the bags sitting by the kitchen door.

Seeing the bags sitting there, he suddenly remembered he had shopped for her. He wanted to talk to her but did not know what to say. Reaching his hand out, palm up, to her, as he had done the first day she had gotten there, he hoped she would place her hand in his. Turning her head to meet his glance, she contemplated the upturned palm. He had made it clear that he wanted nothing to do with her.

Remembering the first day she had arrived, she recognized that he wanted to show her something. She stood and inclined her head, not quite ready to take his hand in hers. Pain and confusion crossed Joe's face. Standing, he took another quick sip of his coffee before tilting his head to the front door. She snagged his keys off the counter before tossing them to him on the way out the door.

In silence, they made their way to the front door. As he went to open it, thunder once more shook the house. She swallowed audibly and tried to shake the fear from her body. Joe reached his hand out to comfort her, but she shied away from his touch, eyes hardening as she looked at him. Reaching past him, she pushed open the front door to see the wind whipping branches across the front lawn.

"There is a storm shelter under the house if it comes to that," Joe stated, inclining his head towards the doors lying against the house. Looking dubiously at them, Hope nodded her head before racing to the side of the jeep. Joe disarmed the car as she opened the door on the back. Seeing the items in the back, she almost squealed in delight. Remembering that Joe was standing there, she did not say a word, simply picked up a paint can in each hand and headed towards the house. She grimaced as the cans dug into her palms, the scrapes from her attack earlier making it difficult to carry. Exasperated, Joe took the cans from her hands and headed to the front porch.

At her gasp, he turned, thinking he had hurt her. A branch had whipped up and sliced her face open. Dropping her gaze, Hope started to get angry. Every time she turned around, she was getting hurt. Storming back to the jeep, she grabbed some of the bags. As she stomped past the jeep door, something yellow caught her eye. Hesitating, she glanced in the passenger side window. Turning to look at Joe, she stopped and pulled open the door. Inside, she found a bouquet of yellow daffodils on the floor of the car. Battered and bruised, yet still beautiful. She started to reach in to pick them up and was startled when she felt Joe push past her and grab them. Picking them up, he slammed the door and marched to the front of the house and up the steps. Tossing the flowers on the rocking chair on the deck, he ran his hand through his hair.

Meanwhile, she took the bags she had grabbed and placed them just inside the door. She picked her way back across the yard to the jeep. This time going around the other side so she could swipe the tear from her cheek without him seeing. Her cheek stung and she was embarrassed thinking that the flowers might have been for her.

It was then that she saw the way the jeep appeared to have slid to a stop outside the house. Turning, she placed her back against the jeep before dropping her head back and closing her eyes. It clicked. Seeing those grooves in the dirt was enough for her to realize how much of a panic he must have been in. She remembered the wild animal she had seen in his eyes when he had found her. A thrill shot through her body to her core at the memory. She suddenly felt a palm on her cheek. She was initially startled until she recognized the touch and the smell of the man in front of her. Drops of rain started to splatter her face. Opening her eyes, she dropped her gaze to Joe's. She could see the pain in his eyes and on his face as he watched her.

He used his thumb to slowly wipe the blood off her cheek. With the advantage of the rain on her face, he watched the rain turn red as it cleaned the wound. When her eyes met his, he pleaded silently with her to let him in. His thumb slowly made its way to her lips; softly rubbing the pad of his thumb on her lower lip, he pulled it down. Her mouth opened on a sigh. When her tongue flicked out to touch the tip, he inhaled quickly. Her eyes flew open on the sound, concerned she had hurt him. Seeing the lust in his eyes, a small smile crept to her lips. Seeing this, Joe placed his other palm on the other side of her face before slowly lowering his mouth to hers. As their lips started to meet, thunder once again crashed across the sky, startling Hope and making her shove Joe back.

Thoroughly embarrassed, she pushed around him to the back of the jeep and grabbed a couple more bags before shutting the door. Making her way up the steps, she was startled when she was suddenly spun around and shoved back against the door. Joe's lips met hers, plundering her mouth with his tongue. Dropping the bags, she raised her arms up and around his neck. When his lips left hers, Hope dropped her head back as his lips made their way down her neck to her shoulder, nipping lightly before suckling slowly. Pulling her shirt aside, he dropped a kiss slowly down her collarbone, stopping just short of the top of her breast. Not wanting to scare her, he made his way back up to her mouth; grabbing her waist, he placed one more crushing kiss on her mouth before reaching behind her and opening the door.

At the feeling of the door opening, Hope dropped her head to Joe's shoulder. Shuddering, she felt his arms wrap gently around her back before pulling her into his arms. "Little One, I will always keep you safe. Never doubt it. And, please, do not leave me again. I don't think I could handle it." Raising her head, she placed a kiss on his cheek before reaching down to pick up the bags she had dropped. Following her inside, he glanced once more out to the ominous sky, hoping that the storm would pass, while selfishly thinking that he would not mind helping Hope feel safe at the sounds of the thunder.

At the ring of his cell phone, Joe glanced down and saw that it was Jelissa. Answering quickly, he heard her explain that she needed him. He watched as Hope's face started to become more shuttered. Grabbing her hand, he brought it to his lips while on the phone listening to Jelissa. Placing a kiss on the inside of her palm, he reassured Jelissa that he would be on his way and to be ready. Hope watched Joe as he ended the call, hope and fear in her gaze. Pulling her palm once more towards him, he surprised her when he bit her wrist before releasing her hand.

"Go run upstairs and get changed, we are going to go pick up Jelissa," Joe instructed softly.

With surprise in her eyes, Hope impulsively leaned forward and kissed him. Expecting it to be a chaste kiss, she was pleasantly surprised when one of his hands dove into her hair and the other pulled her waist to meet his hips. Delving into her mouth with his tongue, he pulled her tightly against him. At her gasp, he gradually released her.

"Do not even think about apologizing," Hope said teasingly. Turning to run up the stairs, she was giddy with excitement, the smack on her butt surprising her. Turning back and seeing Joe, she saw the worry on his face. Knowing that it was instinctual, she called teasingly over her shoulder, "You are going to pay for that."

Chapter 20

Jelissa could see the front of her apartment when the rain began to fall. There was a hitch in her side from practically running the entire way home. She had felt her phone buzz a few times on the way, but she had focused on getting home rather than on her phone. Gasping for breath, she raced up to her front door. She was fumbling for her keys when she realized that she did not have them. She had been so out of sorts from the break-in and Ignoramus that she had not grabbed her keys as she left. She went to reach for the door as her phone rang again. Recognizing the number, she almost did not answer. Grumbling under her breath, she answered the phone. Before she could even speak, she heard a voice say, "Don't go in. It's a trap. Your cat is safe." With that, a click sounded in her ear.

She made a show of looking for her keys and stomping away from the door. Pulling out her phone, she called Karen. When the phone went straight to voicemail, she got worried. Checking her text messages, she saw that she had received a text from Karen saying that there were tornado warnings and she would not be able to make it.

Stunned at the prospect of a tornado coming through, and having nowhere to go, she started to panic. Looking at her phone, she checked again to see if Joe had answered. She was thrilled when she saw that he had answered. There was so much for her to tell him. Calling him, she explained what had happened. Asking for him to come pick her up, since she could not get into her apartment, she hung up the phone when he said he would be on his way. Terrified, she realized that he might not make it in time. Not sure what to do, she sat outside her door shivering in the rain. The overhang above her door did little to protect her from the wind and rain. She sat there for what felt like hours before she heard a car pull up at the end of the sidewalk. Looking up, she saw Joe in his blue Jeep with another person in the back seat. Wary, she waited for him to get out of the jeep.

She watched as he opened his window and, smiling at her, beckoned her to the vehicle. Seeing his face, she remembered what she had felt when she saw him just that morning: safe. Racing to the car, she hopped in as he was shutting the window.

She started to turn to put on her seatbelt when his words stopped her. "You are going to see someone in the back seat. You are not to react. This is extremely important, do you understand?" Looking at him cautiously, she nodded her head. As she turned again to buckle, her eyes met the woman's in the back seat, Hope. She felt her whole body begin to tremble. Turning with a grateful smile on her face, she started discussing the craziness of the weather as they pulled from the lot. Joe started driving through town and started making random turns. When he seemed satisfied, he made a couple of quick turns before heading out of town. He checked his rear-view mirror before looking at Jelissa. "You can react now."

He fully expected her to react positively, to be excited and happy. When she did not say anything, he turned to take in her face. Tears were streaming down her face with the realization that Hope was alive. Turning, she slowly reached out her hand, surprised as she watched Hope recoil. Hurting immensely that she could not give and receive comfort from Hope, she started to turn back around. Joe spoke up, "Hope, please, Little One."

Feeling her courage bolstered by his words, Hope reached forward and took Jelissa's hand.

"It is really good to see you, Aunt Jelissa. I am so sorry for everything that you have gone through due to me. But I am hoping that we can do something to fix that." Glancing up at the rear-view mirror, she caught Joe's eye. His smile of approval lit her up. She could not believe the feeling of safety and contentment that she felt. The wind started picking up even more as they made their way towards the house. Joe flipped on the radio looking for an update on the weather.

"WARNING: THIS IS THE EMERGENCY BROADCASTING SYSTEM. A TORNADO IS EXPECTED TO TOUCH DOWN IN YOUR AREA BETWEEN 5:00 PM AND 6:00 PM. PLEASE MAKE YOUR WAY TO SAFETY. WARNING: THIS IS THE EMERGENCY BROADCASTING SYSTEM. PLEASE MAKE YOUR WAY TO SAFETY."

As they pulled to a stop outside Joe's home, sirens could be heard from the town. As they were hopping out, another car pulled up behind them. Joe immediately pulled out his gun. When he saw his sister, he raced to the car, embracing her before looking over to her passenger seat and seeing Athena. Looking at her gratefully, he called to Hope and Jelissa by their names, rapidly realizing his mistake at Hope's name. His sister smiled wryly and shook her head before helping to unload food, water, and medicine from her car. As they were racing to the double barn doors, they heard everything go still. Looking to the sky, they watched as the clouds started forming into a funnel. Hope raced to the double doors and yanked them open.

Jelissa followed, quickly carrying medicines and water. Joe made his way gingerly down the stairs carrying Athena, doing his very best to not jostle her. When he got to the bottom of the stairs, he saw Hope start to race up. Yelling after her, his voice was snatched away in the wind and she did not hear him. He placed Athena down as quickly as he could and started to head up the stairs, when he caught his sister's glance and she pulled him back. Just as he pulled away and started to go up the stairs, Hope came stumbling in clutching something yellow in her hands. She tried her very best to pull the doors closed. The wind was whipping her hair and the cracked, and potentially broken, ribs from earlier were making it nearly impossible to close.

Joe pulled himself up the steps and helped to pull first one door and then the other closed. Hope quickly placed the brace and stumbled down the stairs. Her hair was littered with debris as she stumbled to stop at the bottom step and simply collapsed. Joe started to reach for her and then remembered that they had an audience. At a loss, he was flummoxed when Hope looked up at him and hurt passed in her eyes. Dropping her gaze, she simply sat, not saying anything. It was Sandra who piped up and said something, "So, Brother, I get the feeling that you and Hope have something going. I'm slightly concerned with the age gap, but I am even more concerned that you seem like you cannot touch her in front of others. Maybe you shouldn't be in a relationship with someone you are too afraid to touch in front of others."

At her words, Jelissa looked sharply from Joe to Hope. Realizing that the statement was true, she started to get upset about the age gap, when she realized that Faith had seen this coming all along. He would have been crazy to not fall for her. The question remained about why he was not wanting to touch her now. Was he ashamed of her? Or simply scared to hurt her? Watching the emotions roll across his face and then the hurt on Hope's, she was going to step in, when Joe suddenly dropped to the bottom step of the stairs and slumped his shoulders.

"I am not ashamed of her..." he began.

"Stop. It's okay, Joe. I know I am not what your sister would wish for you. It was a fantasy. One best forgotten," said Hope as she started to get up when Joe grabbed her hand. Sandra and Jelissa watched silently as she turned to look at him. She was clearly completely at war with herself. Did she cave in and act as though nothing had happened? Or did she make him stand by his promise?

He looked at her desperately, torn between admitting his feelings and possibly endangering his sister or not admitting his feelings and hurting Hope. Fearing what would happen with him and Hope, he did what he felt was best to keep his sister safe.

"She is just someone that I am protecting. That is all. You're right, the age distance is too great, if I even wanted to have a relationship. But, as someone under my protection, that is not something even worth considering at this time." He set his shoulders as he spoke. Glancing quickly at Hope, he watched as her entire face became shuttered. Quickly standing, she went over to Jelissa. Huddling next to her, she started to ask her if she could clean some of the wounds from earlier, whispering quietly to call her Emilia in front of Sandra. It was then that Joe saw why she had run outside: she had grabbed the bouquet of yellow daffodils he had thrown on the porch.

Jelissa wanted to argue, until she thought about how much her life had changed since Hope came into it. She could not blame Joe for wanting to protect his sister. When Hope decided not to argue, Jelissa left it alone. It was not her place to argue. As she started to check on Hope, she turned her back to Sandra and Joe, creating a barrier between Hope and the two. She could hear them muttering to each other behind her back. When there were thumps on the door, they initially disregarded it as debris hitting the doors. When it sounded again, they all looked at each other and realized that someone was out there. Hope stood, pulling her shirt down, and headed towards Joe. Reaching around him, she grabbed his gun out of his waistband and headed up the stairs.

He followed her up the stairs, concerned but knowing that he could not just leave someone out there. Sandra walked up behind them to hold one of the doors closed. Removing the brace, Joe placed his shoulder on the door and started to push, when it was suddenly whipped open from the outside. The face that peeked in startled Joe. He stepped back and allowed the man to help him pull the door closed. Hope watched Joe's face. She saw surprise but not fear, so she put the gun away and briskly made her way down the stairs back to Jelissa. When she looked up and saw Jelissa's face, saw her fear, she drew her weapon all over again.

At his voice, she started trembling in fear. She recognized that voice. One of the many voices that she had heard in her dreams. It terrified her. Joe looked up and saw her with the gun and told her to put it down. Shaking her head no, she looked with fear at the man as he made his way down the stairs. Joe came to her and stood in front of her, calmly placing his hand on the gun and lowering her hand. Turning her eyes from the man behind Joe, she heard Joe's voice. "Little One, put the gun down. I promised you I would keep you safe. You are safe. I promise you. Please, I need you to trust me."

Meeting his eyes, she started to lean into him when she remembered what he had told his sister. Holding the gun out to him by the barrel, she let him take it before turning and walking away. Jelissa stood there, motionless. Seeing the way she stared at the man, Hope realized that she knew him. There was no longer fear, simply confusion and worry. Walking away from all of them, Hope went and laid down on the bed where Athena had been placed. She heard Joe say her name. Without turning, she simply said, "Take care of your sister."

Joe stumbled back from her, realizing that he had broken whatever trust and steps they had made today. Sandra looked from Joe to Hope, then from Jelissa to Henry. Shaking her head, she went to a table placed in the corner and pulled out her book. Immersing herself in the book, she decided to forget the world around her. Glancing up one last time, she saw the way Hope's shoulders were shaking with silent sobs as she lay next to Athena. Looking to Joe, she saw that he was at a loss. He looked at her and met her eyes, determination entering them. Squaring his shoulders, he walked away from Hope.

Standing up, she walked over to Joe and smacked him on the back of the head. Leaning down, she whispered viciously in his ear, "I know that is Hope Matthews. I knew it the first time I saw her this morning. Do not be an idiot and break a good thing. If you care for her simply because she is a victim of that awful ring, then sit over here so she gets used to handling this on her own. If you care for her because of who she is, then get your ass over there. When we leave this horrible hellhole, all I know is that I brought my brother his dog down here, where I always come for tornadoes. I don't know anything about anyone else being down here. Understand?"

Joe turned and met her eyes again. Amazed and then relieved. Of course his sister would know what was going on. Now he needed to decide. Was it simply because she was a victim? Or was it because of who she is? As he deliberated what to do, his sister made her way back over to the chair to read. As the howling became even more extreme outside, he watched her light a lamp in case the power went out. He watched as Henry finally made his way down the stairs to Jelissa. She stood with her arms wrapped around her waist, clearly in a protective stance.

Jelissa was beyond confused about how she should react to seeing Henry enter the storm shelter. He had told her just that morning that he felt nothing, that how she felt was not reciprocated. Seeing him was almost too overwhelming to be able to handle. Between seeing Hope and knowing she was okay, to the relationship between her and Joe, to Henry, she was not sure what to do or where to turn. Wishing she had Nicole, she suddenly remembered the text she had gotten that day about Nicole. At the memory, her legs crumpled beneath her.

Henry caught her before she hit the floor, pulling her up against his body. "What is it?" he questioned. He knew innately that she was not reacting to his appearance with her sobs. Something else had triggered it. The raw pain on her face was enough to break his heart. She had needed him today, had opened herself up, and he had abandoned her. It was with the announcement of the tornado coming that he had decided that she was more important. He had walked off his job. Meredith had watched him leave with approval in her gaze. She knew he was in love with Jelissa and she knew it was reciprocated. She had been able to tell that when she had seen Jelissa in the hospital.

Jelissa looked from Henry to Hope. She knew she needed to tell Hope but was not sure now was the time. Looking to Joe, she mouthed Nicole's name and shook her head as even more tears ran down her cheeks. Henry saw what she had mouthed and pulled her into his arms.

With the knowledge that Nicole was gone, Joe came to the realization that life was too short. He cared for Hope because of who she was. Not because of what happened with her. He got up and made his way to Hope. Seeing that her cries had stopped and she was breathing evenly, he realized she had fallen asleep.

Looking towards Sandra, he indicated she had fallen asleep. Rolling her eyes, she pointed to a blanket. He bent down to pick it up. When he started to lay it on top of her, she cleared her throat. Turning back to look at her, she motioned that he should lay down next to her. His face contorted in pain and fear before he dropped his shoulders. Certain that she would reject him, and knowing that she was terrified of the many things that had been done to her, he started to walk away. It was the whimpering he heard that made up his mind. Bending down to get closer to her, he heard her start trembling and stuttering about a red door, when suddenly she said, "Joe, please help me!"

Reaching down, he lifted Hope from the bed. She lifted her eyes with fear on her face until she saw Joe. Looking past him to his sister, she saw Sandra nod her head, then go back to her book. Turning, she snuggled her head into Joe's chest. She could feel her heart racing. Every time she had tried to go past the red door to the yellow, something was tugging her back. She had a feeling there was something left undone, something that was going to affect her later; however, right now, all she knew was that being held tight by Joe was exactly what she needed.

Joe slowly lowered himself down next to Athena before pulling Hope onto his chest. Her rapid heartbeat and shallow breathing lending to his concern that she was not quite calm from whatever she had been dreaming of. The wind howled overhead and the doors started to shake rapidly. Pulling her close, he saw her glance over to where Henry leaned against the wall with a sobbing Jelissa in his arms. Glancing up at Joe, she asked, "Nicole?"

"I'm sorry, Little One," he answered. With the realization that another woman had been torn from her, Hope tucked her head under his chin, allowing tears to slowly fall from her eyes to his chest. Joe felt his shirt get damp with her tears. Dropping his head back, he brought his arms up around her and waited out the storm. The silent sobs of Jelissa were filling the silence. When the electricity suddenly snapped off, a collective hush filled the room until all that was heard was the wind whipping around outside the doors. In the darkness, they sat, waiting for the calm.

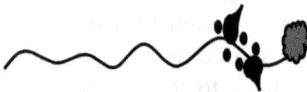

Nicole finished getting Lilly cleaned up and dressed into comfortable clothes. After taking her to the guest bedroom to sleep, she made her way back out to Nate. He sat at the kitchen table with his arms crossed, staring out the window. Walking quietly over to the kitchen sink, she rolled up her sleeves and started washing her hands. She did not realize she was crying until she felt Nate's hands on her arms. Allowing herself the comfort for a moment, she gathered her thoughts and drew in a deep breath. She was surprised that she needed that comfort.

She had seen many horrors. However, this one played too close to home.

When he placed his hands on her arms, he surprised her with the touch, and surprised himself by his willingness to reach out. Usually, he would just leave it alone. He was not willing to open himself up to anyone else. No one else would understand what he did, the torture that he felt with his undercover work. To pretend that he was enjoying what he did was one of the most difficult things he had ever done.

The night he came home from when Lilly had been brought in, the things he had watched and seen were pure torture. Knowing he was being followed by Nicole, he was just the frame to scare her. When he placed her down in his kitchen, he was expecting the harsh words she launched at him. Then, he broke, poured out everything. He was prepared for the disgust. He was prepared for her to hate him, to throw things at him, to want nothing to do with him. It was her reaching out to him that startled him and made him leave the room. He did not deserve someone calling him good. There was nothing good about him. Standing in the kitchen with his hands on her arms, he wanted to offer more comfort, but all he could see were the things he had done. Even grabbing Lilly to convince his partner, James, that the girl was dead but had a good ass.

Expecting Nicole to pull away, he was surprised when she, instead, leaned back against him. Returning the touch without opening herself up. Squeezing her arms one last time, he stepped away, grabbing a hand towel and handing it to her. His phone buzzed suddenly. Looking down, he saw a warning of imminent dangerous weather. Knowing that a call to come into work was possible, he turned to Nicole. She was watching his face as he read the message. When her phone buzzed as well, she realized what was wrong.

"I have a safe room. I know you just got Lilly taken care of, but I will need you to move her downstairs. Lock the door. Do not let anyone in. There is enough food and water down there for two weeks. There are blankets and pillows, as well as a single cot. I am sorry that you will have to sleep on the floor." As he spoke, worry started lacing his words. "If I need to get in, I will know the code. If I come back and cannot seem to get in, do not let me in, no matter what. It will mean that I am not alone. Please do not leave that room for any reason until I come to get you. Can you do that for me?"

Nicole watched his face and realized how serious he was. "What about the girls in the brothel?"

"They are merchandise. The hag will make sure they are protected." With disgust in his tone, he started to turn away.

Nicole grabbed his hand, "Thank you for taking care of us." Squeezing gently, she made her way to the back of the house to wake up Lilly, when she heard a buzz from the front door. Turning back to look at Nate, she saw concern cross his face. She raced back to the kitchen and grabbed her nursing bag. Running to the back, she quickly woke Lilly and hurried with her down the stairs. Getting to the bottom step, she realized that she had no way of getting into the safe room. When the door buzzed open, she saw the camera above the door. Smiling at him, she quickly entered the room and shut the door. It was time to wait.

Chapter 21

The sound of the wind finally died down around 3:00 am in the morning. Joe, Hope, Jelissa, Henry, and Sandra were extremely exhausted from the constant noise of the wind and debris striking the door. Athena was the only one who seemed to have gotten any rest and was the better for it. Her breathing had evened out and she seemed to be resting peacefully. Hope rose her head from Joe's chest when she realized that there was no sound coming in from outside. Turning, she saw that the others had all finally fallen asleep. Worrying that they should not see her on Joe's chest, she started to move, when she felt his arms tighten around her.

"You're not going anywhere, Hope." At his words, she started to lie back down on his chest when his grip on her back became painful. It was growing increasingly tight and she told him it was too tight. Expecting him to release her, she was starting to get worried when his hands only tightened. When his other hand started moving down her body, she asked him to stop. Looking up to try to call Jelissa, she saw Henry, Jelissa, and Sandra standing there staring at her. Watching what he was doing, they refused to be of any help. She started to cry out, begging him to stop.

He started tearing her shirt from her body and running his hands roughly over her skin. Leaving bruises and fear in his wake. When she felt more hands on her, she turned to see that Henry and Jelissa and Sandra had moved over to touch her too, ripping her clothes from her body and tying her hands to the posts on the bed. Underneath her clothes, she found a black and red corset. They seemed to glance over this, taking it in. She fought with everything in her to get away from their prying hands. Suddenly realizing that they would not stop, she started screaming for help.

Gasping, she tried to separate herself from her body, find the yellow door, and make it through the ordeal she was going through. As she started plummeting below the bed, through the floor, and into the earth, she heard a whisper in her ear, "Little One, you are safe, it's me." She recognized the voice of Joe but did not understand why he was trying to hurt her. She had almost made it to the cave, when she suddenly felt lips against hers, soothing and calm. She glanced from the cave to around her and started to calm her breathing. It was only a dream. She was going to be okay.

Allowing Joe's lips and words to bring her to the surface, she woke with the group of people surrounding her as she woke. Joe immediately turned his body, his back to the others, and cradled her against his chest. The wind outside had died down and there seemed to be only an incessant patter of rain hitting the doors. Realizing that they had witnessed her fear, she was extremely embarrassed. Shivering, she wanted to pull away from Joe.

"Hope, please, don't pull away. I have you." She was shocked when she suddenly felt his hand on her lower back. His warm palm resting against the skin of her back, holding her close. It was the first time she had been touched there since she had gotten out. When Joe felt her tense, he realized he was pushing her too fast. Withdrawing his hand, he leaned down and whispered in her ear, "I am removing my hand because I don't want to frighten you. I am not doing it because I don't want to touch you, because I very much want to touch you."

At his words, Hope felt her body get extremely warm all over. Dipping her head, she placed her palm against his chest before snuggling in. She felt his lips press against her hair and she smiled softly to herself. She had been hurt; she had been beaten and raped and broken. The thought of anyone touching her scared her. Yet in Joe's arms she felt safe. She thought about her Aunt Jelissa and Aunt Karen and wondered if she could let them touch her. Nausea hit at the thought and she realized that she would take it one day at a time. It was when the nausea did not pass that she got up quickly from the bed and made it to a bucket in the corner.

Vomiting, she knelt on the floor, hands on the bucket trying to hold herself steady. She felt hands on her shoulder and glanced and saw Jelissa there. Cringing, she tried to pull away while vomiting profusely. Jelissa, seeing her tense, pulled away. Henry watched as Jelissa tried to comfort her. Sandra watched the exchange. She moved to help her when she saw Joe stand and go to Hope. Sitting behind her, he held her hair while she vomited. When she finished, he leaned her back against him. She closed her eyes and tried not to be mortified.

Jelissa was the first to notice the blood on her lips. Wondering what she had gone through to have enough trauma to cause vomiting and blood in the vomit, she went to Sandra, trying to discern what had happened. Hope spoke up, "Aunt Jelissa, I am not deaf, I can hear you." Taking a deep breath, she began. "This morning, Joe left to go to work. He did not want to leave me alone, however, we presumed that I would be safe. He was adamant that I not leave the house, for my own personal safety. However, men figured out where I was and decided to take it upon themselves to find me and hurt me." Swallowing slightly, she smiled in appreciation when Sandra handed her a water bottle.

Taking a small sip, she grimaced as it hit her stomach. Joe rubbed his hand up and down her arm, waiting for her to continue, he had yet to hear what had happened. "I was upstairs, had just finished taking a shower, when I remembered that Joe was giving me full reign of his house. It was exciting. I have always wanted to work on an old home. I started to head down the stairs when I heard someone down there." Joe's hands tensed on her arms at her words. Reaching up, she placed her palm on his cheek. Tilting her head back, she placed a kiss on his chin.

"I got down the stairs before I was knocked flat on my butt in laughter. It was Athena, she had used her mouth to open the room she had been locked in. She was so excited and proud of herself. She jumped on me and started licking my face! It was amazing and it felt great to do something so carefree. I grabbed the memo pad off the counter and started deciding what I was going to do, um, to your house." As she finished, her voice trailed off and she laughed nervously.

Chuckling, Joe dropped a kiss on the top of her head. Henry took a seat on the floor to listen, pulling Jelissa between his open legs and wrapping his arms around her. Sandra sat back down at the table, eager to listen to what Hope was saying.

"Anyway, I had been sitting on the couch in the living room when Athena suddenly lifted her head from my knee and started growling…"

"Wait, she was up on the couch?" Joe interjected.

"There is a strong possibility that I invited her up onto the couch with me." Looking up at him and grinning, she continued her story. "It was the growl that alerted me that there might be a problem. She started herding me through the house before shoving me to the kitchen door. We hit the porch just as I heard the front door kicked in. We were already racing through the yard towards the trees when I realized that I had no shoes on and only the bath robe. I never intended to sit so long. A man tackled me to the ground and shot Athena. Then…" her voice trailed off. Looking desperately at Joe, she pleaded silently with him to not have to finish her tale.

"Suffice it to say that when I found her, I was not happy with the predicament I found her in and shot the three men. I have no idea if they are alive or dead, and I honestly do not care. After I shot the three men, we got Hope and Athena to my sister, Sandra, put Hope in bed, and then went to get Jelissa after letting Hope rest for a bit." Pulling Hope close, they both relived the parts they had not said. Joe felt Hope tense and wondered what she was thinking. Was it about the men standing over her, ripping the robe from her body? Was it him telling her to leave? She had reacted harshly to what he had said, however, she had been through a lot. Looking to Jelissa to see her reaction to their day, he finally noticed the protective way that Henry was holding her. It was then that he saw the bruises on her neck.

"Your turn, Jelissa. What happened? Who do I need to kill?" Joe intoned, completely deadpan.

Henry quickly interjected, "Get in line. What happened, pet? Who hurt you?"

Joe glanced sharply at Henry, expecting that he already knew what had happened. "My house was thrashed. No, I do not know who it was." Jelissa leaned her head back against

174

Henry's chest, resting her forehead against his cheek. Closing her eyes, she relived the horror of discovering her home and what happened when Ignoramus and Nate had gotten there. When Henry heard that Nate had not stopped him until damage had already been done, he grew tense. Jelissa felt him tense and did not fault him for it. Not sure she would ever forgive Nate for allowing his partner to assault her, she continued up until the point that she got to the hospital. At the completion of her recounting her day, Henry wrapped his arms around her before grabbing her chin and tilting her head to his. His lips met hers in a branding no one could question.

As he pulled away, he whispered fiercely, "I love you. No one will ever touch you like that ever again." Jelissa's eyes widened at his words before a calm swept across her features.

Turning, she looked at him, love apparent on her face. Sandra, Hope, and Joe felt they were intruding on their moment and turned their back. Sandra returned to her book, while Joe once again cradled Hope to his chest. He could feel that she had pulled away emotionally but did not feel that he could mend that bridge at this time.

It was the multitude of emotions roiling through him that gave him pause. His sister was right: there was a large age difference. Hope had been through an extremely rough time. While he knew he cared for her, she still had such a long journey ahead of her. Would it make more sense for him to just be her support and nothing more? With that thought, he slowly started to extricate his arm from under her head. When she saw him start to pull away, she caught his eye. Seeing his determination, she got up and walked back to the bed before once more curling up against Athena.

In his mind, he saw the way he had found her. The men crowding around her, prepared to defile her before returning her to the brothel. He did not know how they had found her and, therefore, did not know how he could prevent it from happening again. Sitting up, he ran his hands through his hair, scrubbing his face with the dilemma of where she could go where she would be safe, and not just from those from the brothel but from him as well.

Nicole did the best she could to keep track of the days that she and Lilly were stuck in the safe room. It was hard to tell when a day had passed, because there was no light from the outside. The power had been knocked out within hours of them ending up in the room. She had not heard anything from above, so she did not know if the storm had passed and how much damage had been done. The generator appeared to be one that would turn on when power was required then shut back off if there was not enough of a draw. It was strange, almost like a compressor, however, it had allowed her to time it. The generator had kicked on, pushing fresh air into the room. She had timed it to about every three hours that it would kick on. This was how she tracked the days. On the sixth day, she and Lilly were starting to get cabin fever.

Not understanding why Nate was not there to let them out, she started to wonder if he had been hurt or if there was too much debris and he could not get to them. Lilly became more and more secluded the more she stayed down here alone. She stated at one point that she had gone from one prison to the other. At least in the other, she had the hope that someone was looking for her. Now, she figured no one would even notice she was gone. She sank further and further into depression.

Nicole did her best to try and pull her out of her funk, but her efforts only seemed to alienate her more. She tried cuddling, anger, love, empathy, and silence. Nothing seemed to make it better, if anything, she made it worse. Some of the wounds that had been inflicted on her started to get dirty and infection started to set in. When Nicole tried to fix it, Lilly would push her away. At a loss, she watched as the wounds continued to fester until they stank. Exasperated, she finally told Lilly that she had to let her clean them for her own sanity. Looking Nicole dead in the eye, she told her to get over it, then went back to staring at the wall.

Nicole spent her time from then on trying to keep herself active and busy. Sit-ups and push-ups became a part of her daily routine, jumping jacks soon joined in. There was little water, until on the sixth day, when she started to go out of her mind and decided to explore. Leaning against a wall, she found a lever that seemed to open another room, she pushed and prodded. Upon the wall sliding open, she rolled her eyes. Inside, she found stores upon stores of water and food. There was a shower and a mini-gym. Dropping her head to the door, she was filled with mirth at herself for not being nosy earlier.

She was startled from her mirth when she suddenly heard laughter coming from behind her. "All this time, we could have had more space and not felt like we had to do everything in front of the other. Next time, I am not being polite. I am going to be nosy. I call the shower," Lilly spouted. As she left the small room where they had stayed, Nicole stood open-mouthed at her enthusiasm for a shower. Closing the hidden door most of the way, she sat on the floor outside, embarrassed and confused. She was worried about Nate and where he was. She was worried about Jelissa and Karen and Joe. She missed Hope and wished she could have helped her.

Hearing a scream from the other room, Nicole rushed in to find Lilly standing in terror as a man loomed down on her. Nicole recognized him as Nate's partner. Not understanding how he had gotten in there, she ran for a weight in the corner of the room and slammed it against the back of his head. As he crumpled, she saw that the lecherous man had pulled himself free of his pants and it appeared that he had been intending to rape Lilly. As she stood staring at him, Lilly ran up and kicked him in the head and then the stomach, before falling next to him and pummeling him with her fists.

Nicole finally came to her senses and pulled Lilly off him. She did not know why Lilly hated him so much, but after seeing what he looked ready to do to Lilly, she could guess. After removing her from him, she told Lilly to go to the other room and get her medical bag. Lilly, looking angrier than Nicole had ever seen her, ran to the other room. Bringing back the bag, she deposited it on the back of the man's head. Nicole simply thanked her, then rummaged through it until she found something she could use to knock him out. Quickly inserting a needle into his arm, she waited and checked his pulse. Pulling him to the corner, she was straightening when she heard the outer door open.

Shoving Lilly into the shower, she closed the secret door and waited for the person on the other side to come in. She heard nothing until, suddenly, the door started to creep open. "Nicole, please tell me you are in here!" she heard a voice yell.

Nicole, recognizing the voice, realized that it was Nate. He walked into the room as Nicole walked over to him. Seeing his partner on the floor, fear crossed his features. "I wondered where he had gone. He was supposed to meet me at the station the other night and never showed. Then, the tornado hit and I have been dealing with the injured. Are you okay?" Before she even had the opportunity to answer, he suddenly spun around. "Where is Lilly?" he gasped out fervently.

Stepping out from the shower, Lilly saw Nate standing there. "I am still here. Why are you concerned about where I am after the things you let them do to me?"

Nicole inhaled deeply at the words, confounded that Lilly would bring that up after he had used his safe room to care for them the last few days.

"Because I am merely human. I care, because it is what I do. I let them do those things to you because I could not find a way to get you out of the situation that you were in without getting one or both of us killed. I hate myself every day for what happened to you. And I will spend as much time as I need to do things to show you that I would never have left you there that long if I felt I had a choice." Nate turned to meet Nicole's eyes. He could tell she wanted to speak out. Shaking his head quickly, he turned to his partner.

"What happened to James? Did he hurt you?" Nate asked the women standing before him.

"No, he did not hurt us, Lilly saw to that. I have given him a sedative. He should be out for the next eight hours, at least," Nicole answered quickly. Nate nodded his head at this before going and lifting James off the floor. Carrying him out of the room, he glanced back long enough to say, "Lilly, feel free to use the shower, and, uh, Nicole, you smell like ass, you should take one too." Winking quickly at Nicole, he left the room. Astonished at what he had said to her, Nicole felt her jaw drop. She was suddenly surrounded by the sound of the most

178

beautiful and contagious laughter she had ever heard, filling the room. Turning, she caught Lilly smiling enthusiastically at her. Laughing along with her, Nicole headed out the door. When she saw that he had shut and locked the room, she almost screamed. Then, realizing it was only for her safety, she started pulling clothes out of her bag for both her and Lilly to change into.

Waiting, she was surprised when, five minutes later, she heard the door start to open again. Nate stepped back in. Seeing her sitting on the cot, he was grateful she had been there and able to get to this safe room. A tree had fallen onto his roof and smashed into the room she and Lilly would have been staying in. Luckily, the rest of his house was not too damaged and insurance would be able to cover it. He was also extremely exhausted. Nicole noticed him staring, then watched as he swayed. Quickly standing, she pulled a clean blanket off a pile and laid it down on the cot. Turning, she walked to him and grabbed his arm, tugging him down until he lay on the cot.

Looking at her gratefully, he started to close his eyes. "Please do not leave until I wake. I need to know you're okay. I mean, that the both of you can get out okay." Shaking his head, he tossed his arm over his eyes and started to lightly snore. Waiting her turn, she was pleased when Lilly shut off the shower about ten minutes later. Nicole walked in and handed her a clean towel and her clothes. Asking her to wait for her, she made Lilly promise that she would not go anywhere without her.

Stepping into the shower, Nicole wondered at the man sleeping in the other room.

Chapter 22

Karen felt her life slip back into a routine. She had received a text from Jelissa after the tornado simply stating that 'she could still hope, for it had not died that night.' At first misunderstanding, she had started to text back, when she realized what that meant. Hope had not died that night after all. She did not know what had happened yet, but the elation she felt was enough to make her feel like she could, once more, make a difference in the lives of others around her. She went to Hope and Faith's home and started watering plants and cleaning. She wanted it to be ready for when Hope came home. She was elated that she would be able to help Hope have all her dreams come true.

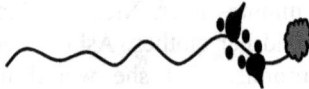

Nate decided, when he woke to find Lilly and Nicole in his safe room, that he needed to do something different with his life. He refused to continue to allow these women to be hurt while he stood by and watched. He would ask Nicole and Lilly to move in with him.

Encouraging Nicole to contact her friends, he told her that it was time they took a stance. Every day that he spent with her, he realized that he was developing feelings for her. Sure, she could never accept him as he was, so he did everything in his power to become what she would want. Eating healthier, exercising, only having a glass of wine when she would have a glass, he started changing his ways.

He watched as Lilly slowly fell into a routine. She seemed extremely out of it the majority of the time. However, he and Nicole did not know what they could do to make this change. They did what they could to make her feel safe and accepted. They had even contacted the friend who had reported her missing. However, when the friend showed up and saw the damage that had been done, and realized that she was a victim of rape, she wanted nothing to do with her. She left saying that Lilly must have done something to draw that kind of attention to herself. Lilly had locked herself in her room after that.

Nicole spent every day trying to find a way to make a difference after the tornado had struck. She and Nate had spoken about contacting her friends, but she was terrified for their lives. Deciding that she wanted to get a firmer idea of what she would like to do to help, she started writing in a journal all the ideas that she had. She noticed that Nate seemed to be changing his routine, and she was pleased with the changes she was seeing. She felt indebted to him for everything that he had done, saving her and saving Lilly. Thinking of Lilly made her feel as though she was doing something wrong, and she did not know how to help her.

Realizing that Lilly had been exceptionally angry and wanting to help, Nicole decided to find her and see if she would have any ideas about how to prevent the ring from continuing their destructive behavior. Going to her room, she knocked on the door multiple times. When she did not answer, she called her name a few times. She heard rustling on the other side of the door. Concerned, she called for Nate before trying to turn the knob, she was met with resistance. The door was locked. Nate came around the corner and saw the panic on her face. He quickly reached above the door frame and grabbed down a key. Turning the key in the lock, they rushed into the room. Not seeing Lilly, they rushed to the bathroom, praying they would find her there. When they entered the bathroom, they found Lilly sitting in the corner, eyes starting to glaze. Her wrists ran red with blood where she had cut them with a pair of scissors. Hope immediately grabbed towels to halt the flow. Losing consciousness, Lilly slumped forward. Nate looked to Nicole, and in silent agreement, they headed to the car to take her to the hospital. Fear filling both of them with the potential repercussions of being seen together, but they needed to save her life.

Joe woke to the sound of panic coming from Hope as she slept, her pitiful cries resonating through him as she fought her own terror. In the week since the tornado, they had seldom touched, let alone talked. He heard her struggle through the dream, crying out in terror. He did not know what she saw in those dreams and could not get her to talk about them.

The first night the dream happened, Joe had attempted to comfort her and she had clammed up and pushed him away. Running to the bathroom, she had gotten sick. Not understanding why she was so disgusted by him, they quickly had moved to not speaking. In the mornings, he still got himself ready first and made her a tray with tea and toast. However, of late, she did not even touch the tray.

Hope suddenly sat up in bed and screamed. He heard a door slam open down the hall and Henry and Jelissa came running. Jelissa had not felt that going home was safe after the phone call she had received, and Henry's home had been demolished from the tornado.

Joe figured he could handle one more week with them there before he completely lost his mind. It was not that he did not appreciate them being there, he just did not appreciate them constantly, well, being there. He sat up on the couch in his room and gently placed his feet on the floor. Steepling his fingers, he placed his chin on his fingers and watched them once more smother Hope. Hope shied away from their touch every time they came in, the mortification on her face was enough that Jelissa and Henry should have realized what was happening. They were not making things better by rushing into the room to 'save' her, they were making it worse. Jelissa sat down on the edge of the bed and tried to comfort Hope. When she reached out to pull her into her arms, Joe watched the panic consume her face.

"Enough!" he shouted. "Get out of my room and do not come back in unless you are invited in. You are guests in my home, and I am fine with you being here, but you are not welcome in my room anymore. Is that understood?" Jelissa and Henry looked at Joe like he had completely lost his mind.

"We are only trying to make sure my niece is okay. Maybe if you'd let me buy her a bed, she wouldn't have to be here and we wouldn't be barging into your room," Jelissa scolded. By now, Hope had shrunk back against the headboard, hating herself for being the cause of so much strife. She had ideas for what she could do to help the other girls. She wanted to help them get out of the brothel and be safe. However, she could not even get these people, who cared for her, to leave her alone. She watched as Joe stood from the couch, her eyes immediately dropping to his bare stomach, it made her mouth water and her heart race. In her mind, she knew he would never hurt her, at least not physically, but the fear of being touched, especially with her being what she was starting to suspect, was not even a possibility. Anticipating the argument that was about to ensue, Hope started to raise her hand.

Joe watched as Hope's eyes went wide when he stood, and she seemed to swallow quickly. Disgusted with himself for scaring her by yelling, he wanted to stop but could not back down. When Hope rose her hand to stop them from speaking, it was the final straw. "No, Hope. Not this time!" his voice lashed across the room, making Hope flinch and recoil. Jelissa stood, not happy with Joe for snapping at Hope.

Before she could even speak, Henry's voice broke the stunned silence of the room, "Pet, it's time to go back to our room. Leave it alone for now. The man has a point." Walking forward, he grasped Jelissa's arm and pulled her from the room. She was not pleased at being remanded by both Joe and Henry and was not happy that Hope was so afraid.

Getting back to their room a few doors down, Henry pulled her into the room before slamming her against the door and ravaging her mouth with his. When he finally broke away with a gasp, Jelissa huffed quickly and said, "You know, you don't get to solve every argument between us by kissing me."

"Don't I?" he returned. Dragging her to the bed they had set up just the morning before, he tossed her back on the bed, latching her wrist to a cuff before she even had time to react. Surprised yet intrigued, she grew quiet and watched. He had only hinted before of the things he liked to do in the bedroom. She wondered if tonight she would finally get a demonstration. He walked around the bed, slowly attaching her legs to silk binds on the base of the bed and then cuffing her other hand to the headboard. Shivering despite not being cold, Jelissa watched Henry as he prowled around her.

They had spoken about the group of private investigators that he had actually worked for. While not an off-the-books organization as he had initially said, leading to many arguments, it was designed specifically to break up sex trafficking rings, child pornography groups, and solve child abduction cases. They operated just on the outskirts of the law, many times getting results by not waiting for a search warrant or a go from a superior. They were paid vigilantes. Her attention was drawn back to him, suddenly, when he approached the bed. He leaned down as though he was going to kiss her, when she suddenly felt a blindfold cover her eyes. "Henry!" she gasped.

"Don't make a sound unless you want me to gag you," he answered quickly. Catching her breath, she waited. Silence descended on the room and she waited, straining to hear what was happening. The seconds turned to minutes and she started twisting against the binds. She heard the door open and close. Wanting to ask who that was, she started to speak when she remembered his directions. Straining in the silence to hear something, anything, she was startled when she heard the door open again.

Her body grew taut as she waited for some movement. When she suddenly felt his hand push her shirt up her stomach, exposing her skin, her chest rose and fell quickly as the anticipation built. Gasping, she felt something extremely cold get placed on her stomach, her muscles contracting from the cold. He lazily drew circles around her stomach, the ice cube in his hand leaving a trail of water glistening on her skin. Unable to resist, he leaned down and followed the trail of the ice cube with his tongue. Laving at her belly button with his tongue, her quick intake of breath persuaded him to continue.

Jelissa writhed against the bindings, needing to touch, to see. Unable to do either of those things, her sense of feeling was heightened to an almost intolerable level. Arching her body, she tried to get closer to his mouth and hands as he caressed her body. His hands firm, then soft, rough, then tender. Overwhelmed, needing him to touch more, she whimpered. At the sound, he stopped touching her completely. A sigh escaped her body as trepidation filled her. He said to not make a sound. Startled, she heard his voice.

"Jelissa, my pet, what is your safe word?" he grew silent, waiting for her answer. He technically had not given her permission to speak. Would she obey or would she answer? Henry watched as her breathing turned to quick pants. He quickly noted her brow and saw that, rather than anticipation, there were creases of anxiety. Leaning forward quickly, he placed his lips gently against hers. "You have done well, pet. You may answer the question," he whispered against her lips.

Gasping with him so near, she thought for a moment before quirking her lips. "Quarter. My safe word is quarter." At her words, Henry, at first, was confused until he remembered the day she had dropped a quarter in the store parking lot to distract him from Joe. A smile crossed his lips. Unable to help himself, he crushed his lips to hers, humbled that she was his. As he pulled away, she breathed, "I love you." As her words escaped her lips, he watched as her body went taut. This time in worry.

"My pet, this is something that you never need permission to say. I love you too, with every part of who I am, with every part of who I will be, and with every part of what and who we will be together." After each reason, he placed a kiss to her forehead, then her nose, her chin, and finally her mouth. She tentatively reached up with her tongue to rub it along his lips. Groaning in pleasure, Henry returned the kiss before standing. "So, we begin." At his words, he pulled a knife from the side table and approached Jelissa.

After Jelissa and Henry left the bedroom, Joe looked to Hope. She no longer had fear on her face, simply worry. He crossed to the bedroom door and shut and locked it. Something he had never done before, because he did not want her to feel trapped. Turning to look at her, she cocked her head sideways before a single word slipped from her mouth, surprising both of them, "Finally."

Certain that he had misheard her, he did not respond. Walking back to the couch, he started to sit down when, suddenly, Hope got up and ran to the bathroom, getting violently ill once again. Joe started to leave it, to not say anything to her. However, Jelissa and Sandra both had said that she should no longer be vomiting blood. He needed to know if she was so that he could get her proper medical attention. Walking calmly into the bathroom, he snagged a hairband off the counter and walked over to her.

Without bothering to ask for permission, he ran his fingers through her hair, pulling it back into a ponytail. Surreptitiously glancing into the toilet, he saw that there was no blood. Presuming that this was simply stress from everything that had happened, he was determined to get things as far back to normal as he could.

That would start with him getting Henry and Jelissa out of his house. He had never minded people around before, but he still remembered the way that Henry had behaved the first time he had shown up with Hope, with the hood over her face. Unsure he would ever forgive him for that, he started to stand, when he felt her lean back, trembling, against him. "I am sorry, I know you do not want me touching you. If you could just help me lean against the wall, you can be on your way. Thank you for putting my hair up." At her words, Joe tensed. Deciding that it was not worth the battle, he moved her against the wall and shut the toilet, flushing the vomit as quickly as he could, he hated that smell. Reopening the toilet, he started to walk out. Turning back, he saw that she had laid her head back against the wall, arms limply hanging by her sides.

Grabbing a washcloth, he started to wet it, when he heard her voice one more break the silence between them. "You know, if touching me disgusts you so much that you cannot even touch me without washing your hands, maybe I should go

somewhere where my disgusting self cannot contaminate you."
As she spoke, Joe's body started to shake with fury. She had
been dumped on him with no warning. He had no idea who was
going to be entering his home. He had given her his favorite
pair of sweatpants and allowed her to use his bed. He had been
sleeping on a couch since she arrived and was extremely sore.
It was not like his 6'3" frame could easily fit on the couch. Not
to mention, he was not even washing his hands, had not even
considered washing his hands. For her to throw that in his face
was absolutely ridiculous.

"Open your eyes, Hope, and look at me," he said firmly.
When he saw that she had opened her eyes and saw the
washcloth in his hands, he tossed the rag to her. "I don't know
where this 'pity me' party is coming from, but I want no part of
it. If you are not happy here and do not want to be here, then
leave. But please do not pretend like the reason you are leaving
is because of anything that I am doing. You have made the
decision time and time again to pull away. You realize that you
are in my home, right?" As he continued to spew his words,
Hope shrank further and further into herself, ashamed of how
she was treating him.

"Joe," she started.

"No, I am not finished. You will listen to me. It is my turn
to speak and your turn to listen, for once. You think that
walking away is really going to solve anything? You think that
when I look at you or touch you, I am disgusted? Well, guess
what? You're right!"

As his sentence finished, Hope felt her last bit of happiness
fade. She had finally started feeling like maybe she had the
potential to become who she wanted to be. Without even
realizing it, silent tears started filling her eyes and spilling
down her cheeks. Joe continued pacing back and forth in the
small space, completely oblivious to the effect he was having
on Hope.

"Every time I look at you, I see an 18-year-old girl who got
dealt a shitty card in life. You were taken on your first day of
school. Your senior year. You should be planning homecoming
right now, your senior ball, or some other nonsense. You
should be applying to universities and deciding where you will
go and what major you want to have, but, instead, here you sit

in my bathroom. You should be going to parties and getting drunk and making out with your boyfriends in the back of their cars, and yet you sleep here, in my bed, alone.

Every time I look at you, I see a potential that is no longer there. Every time I look at you, I see what could have been and, instead, has been broken and bruised. I see what has been stripped away from you and I am disgusted." His words were falling, one after the other, with no consideration of the consequences. He was tired of being silent, tired of stepping on eggshells around her.

As Hope sat listening to everything that Joe was saying, the desperation she had felt to be accepted and maybe even loved by someone broke down even further than she thought possible. She would never be seen as anyone other than a victim. Determination raced down her spine to make a difference, to do something different. Never again would she put herself in the position to be treated this way.

"Joe, are you done? I think it is my turn," Hope interjected. At her words, Joe heard the catch in them, turning, he saw her face, saw the tears that she had yet to wipe away. Anger filled his face when he realized that this entire situation was such a mess.

"No, I am not done. Let me finish what I have to say," Joe responded. Closing his eyes, he drew in a deep breath before starting to speak again. The smell of daffodils suddenly struck his nose again. He saw a yellow door in his mind's eye. He felt a pull towards it but thought it ludicrous and, instead, opened his eyes, the smell of daffodils staying in the back of his senses. "You were a pretty girl who had every possibility in front of her. You would have probably been the most popular girl at that school. And, yet, here you sit.

It seems like every time you turn around, you are getting hurt. Here is the catch, though. And this is where it gets absolutely grand." Drawing a deep breath, he plunged ahead, "I can't imagine you being anywhere but here in this house with me. Before you got here, it was just a monstrosity that I could not stand. Now, there are subtle changes throughout. From the small things, like a hairband on the counter, to the bigger things, like the bathroom downstairs that you are painting yellow. When I think of where you would be the safest, the only place I can see you is here, sitting at the bar in the kitchen, sitting up in my bed after a nightmare has had the unfortunate circumstance of invading that wickedly beautiful head of yours.

When I look at you and see the beautiful woman that you have become and see the shitty card that you have been dealt, all I want to do is make sure that you are never dealt such an awful card ever again. I want to protect you and keep you from those things in your life. I know that you have the ability to go to school and become popular and have boyfriends. But every time I think of any other man or, in this case, boy touching you, I can't imagine doing anything other than ripping their hands off for touching you."

As Joe continued to speak, Hope was astounded by the things that he was saying. How could this beautiful, strong, loyal man ever feel the things that he was saying? Especially for a woman like herself.

"Do you know why I am disgusted when I look at you, Hope? Not because of you or anything that has happened to you, but rather because I am not some teenage boy with a crush. I am a grown man who thinks of doing things to you that are so beyond anything that you should experience at this age. Then, I think that many of these things have already been done. Then, I want to kill those people for taking these things from you and for not letting me be the first to show you the pleasures that can be found. I am falling for you. Every day, I fall even further. I can feel my fingertips barely gripping the edge of this huge chasm. Once I let go…" his voice trailed off here.

Looking at her desperately, he realized how much he had just said and what it could mean if she did not answer him in kind. He had literally just laid his heart out for her to see. He was suddenly hit with what felt like a sledgehammer to his chest. He loved her. He had already taken the plunge. Would she be there to fall with him, or was it too soon?

Hope listened in wonderment as he spoke, desperate to be able to reciprocate his feelings. She hated being touched now by anyone unless it was him. When she thought of where she wanted to be every day, it was with him by her side. He was right: she still had so much of her life left to live, but she could not imagine living it without him. She would graduate from high school, but then she had other plans. Looking at his face, she saw how much he truly cared. She decided to take the plunge with him, to tell him that she could not imagine a life without him.

She smiled as she thought of how to tell him. Seeing this, Joe felt relief course through his body. Reaching over, he lifted her up and kissed her, kissed her with a passion he had only dreamed of showing her. When she suddenly started pushing away from him, he grew confused and released her. She immediately dropped to her knees in front of the toilet, getting sick again. Joe was devastated. She was truly disgusted by him. He grabbed the washcloth off the floor, rinsed it, and placed it next to her. It was as he was walking out of the bathroom that her voice stopped him cold in his tracks, "Wait, Joe, it's not you. I've been trying to find a way to tell you. I'm pregnant."

www.ingramcontent.com/pod-product-compliance
Lightning Source LLC
Chambersburg PA
CBHW050119280326
41933CB00010B/1165